Management Ethics

The Palgrave Macmillan IESE Business Collection is designed to provide authoritative insights and comprehensive advice on specific management topics. The books are based on rigorous research produced by IESE Business School professors, covering new concepts within traditional management areas (Strategy, Leadership, Managerial Economics) as well as emerging areas of enquiry. The collection seeks to broaden the knowledge of the business field through the ongoing release of titles, with a humanistic focus in mind.

MANAGEMENT ETHICS

Placing Ethics at the Core of Good Management

Domènec Melé

Professor and Holder of the Chair of Business Ethics, IESE Business School, University of Navarra, Spain

First published 2012 by
PALGRAVE MACMILLAN

Palgrave Macmillan in the UK is an imprint of Macmillan Publishers Limited, registered in England, company number 785998, of Houndmills, Basingstoke, Hampshire RG21 6XS.

Palgrave Macmillan in the US is a division of St Martin's Press LLC, 175 Fifth Avenue, New York, NY 10010.

Palgrave Macmillan is the global academic imprint of the above companies and has companies and representatives throughout the world.

Palgrave® and Macmillan® are registered trademarks in the United States, the United Kingdom, Europe and other countries

ISBN-13: 978-0-230-24630-0

This book is printed on paper suitable for recycling and made from fully managed and sustained forest sources. Logging, pulping and manufacturing processes are expected to conform to the environmental regulations of the country of origin.

A catalogue record for this book is available from the British Library.

A catalog record for this book is available from the Library of Congress.

10 9 8 7 6 5 4 3 2 1
21 20 19 18 17 16 15 14 13 12

Printed and bound in Great Britain by
CPI Antony Rowe, Chippenham and Eastbourne

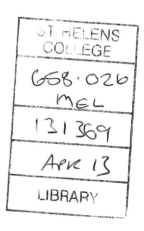

CONTENTS

PREFACE

Management ethics is generally understood as morality in relation to the practice of management. This book focuses on this subject, paying particular attention to its foundations and how ethics should be placed at the core of good management.[1] This book does not seek to offer a list of the best ethical practices in management, nor to consider the ethical issues commonly found in management,[2] although some of these matters will also receive our attention. The main concern of this book is to gain an understanding of the relationship between ethics and management and to discuss some basic ethical requirements for good management.

For many years "good ethics is good business" has been an often repeated maxim. In this way some have tried to convince managers and business people that ethics are profitable in the long run. The words were echoed in the 1980s, when Kenneth H. Blanchard and Norman V. Peale published their successful book entitled *The Power of Ethical Management*.[3] The basic argument of the authors was that it has been frequently demonstrated that the sacrifice of a short-term advantage will lead to a better long-term result in terms of both profitability and ethical aspiration.

Most reviewers of this book agreed with their view, but James W. Hathaway, a professor of management, wrote a review which, without denying the influence of ethics on long-term results, pointed out that the real problem was not convincing the audience of this, but the persistence of attraction found in the short-term: "as shown in many of today's headlines, the short-run gains are proving so often to be irresistible".[4] This may be true not only in investors but also in business executives who often are pressured to act driven by short-term results. These pressures are not necessarily a threat, but can adopt the form of strong incentives to favor short-term results through bonuses or stock options or other means aligned with quarterly earnings.

In the first decade of the 21st century we have learned a lot about the moral consequences of such incentives from the subprime crisis, which not only brought about the bankruptcy of Lehman Brothers and others, but resulted in dramatic repercussions on a global scale. Moreover, examples of mismanagement with a notorious lack of ethics have been abundant in recent years, often with awful consequences; Arthur Andersen, Enron, Welcome, Parmalat, Madoff, are just a few that might spring to mind.

Although certain counter-arguments can be found,[5] the feeling that ethics contributes to long-term results continues to have currency, and many recognize the beneficial power of ethical management. This book takes the same position, but it emphasizes that management should take ethics into account because management is about people and dealing with people requires ethics. A business firm is not like a machine, nor like a biological organism driven by physical or biological laws. A business firm is, first of all, a human reality. Those who run the firm are conscious and free persons who cooperate within an organization with common goals. Decisions and actions of the manager are human decisions and actions which will serve or damage people, including the manager him or herself. Thus, ethics is not an artificial add-on to management, it is an intrinsic dimension of good management.

There is no doubt that good management entails being efficient, but this is only the "technical" side of management. Managers need people to achieve goals and it is through people that management can be efficient. If management mistreats these people, does not respect their dignity and rights, or prevents their growth as human beings, it is not fully good management.

Ethics are also necessary for good management because of their influence on efficiency. We know that efficient management that produces good economic performance depends on many factors, including technology, structure and processes, communication, motivation and leadership. The contribution of these factors to efficiency is not only a matter of their technical quality, but also one of willingness of those involved in the organization to work and cooperate, and underlying this willingness are trust and morale. Trust, morale and willingness to cooperate can be eroded or even jeopardized if collaborators feel manipulated, or overlooked, or maybe treated unjustly in some other way.

Ethics is different from efficiency but the two are interdependent. Having an ethical sense pushes one to be responsible and to act in the best way for the purposes of efficiency. In turn, efficiency in a business firm is a contribution to the common good. An efficient use of means provides material support to human life and better accessibility to economic goods. Through increasing competitiveness, efficiency also contributes to maintaining jobs, so providing the livelihood of many people.

Ideas about the contribution of ethics to good management are extended in Chapter 1 of this book, along with further considerations and arguments. We argue that ethics is embedded in management through managerial decision-making, through ideas and values (ethos) which drive the practice of management, and also through the manager's moral character. This chapter uses an intuitive notion of ethics, but for the purposes of the book a deeper understanding of ethics is required. This is the aim of Chapter 2, where we focus on basic ethics for managers. We avoid sophisticated philosophical considerations, but try to explain some fundamental points of ethics with rigor. We explain that ethics is sometimes understood in a very narrow sense, as a mere tool for solving dilemmas and as a constraint in decision-making. To counter this, the book assumes a sense of ethics taken from the philosophy of Ancient Greece, which presents ethics as a guideline for moral excellence. From this perspective, ethics do much more than introduce prohibitions; they focus on choosing the best possible moral alternative in each situation.

The following chapters focus on three basic topics, the importance of which for good management is discussed in Chapter 1. One is ethics in decision-making, which is the topic of Chapter 3. This chapter pays special attention to the necessity for a holistic approach to decision-making, considering the results pursued, possible reactions, the internal learning of the decision-maker and ethical evaluation. How to make a sound moral judgment for decision-making is widely developed in this chapter.

Chapters 4 and 5 consider the second topic, the ethos of management – the ideas and values which drive the practice of management. Views of the individual, the firm and the purpose of business in society, are the subject matter of these chapters. Chapter 4 discusses what might be an appropriate view of the human individual and the business firm, and the centrality of the person in management is suggested, after discussing the richness of the notion of "person". This demands appropriate treatment in dealing with people beyond the well-known reasons related to performance and profitability. Reflecting on human characteristics and on the nature of the firm leads us to suggest that the business firm is a community of persons with a specific mission; and not as a mere organization based on a set of contracts or interests. This view requires a consistent way of using managerial power and of managing organizational structure and systems.

Chapter 5 reflects on the purpose of business in society and its corresponding responsibilities and accountability. Far from seeing the purpose of the firm only in economic terms, with the only responsibility being to make profits or increase the share value, the chapter presents the business firm as an actor which contributes to the common good and to sustainable development by creating wealth and knowledge efficiently, providing responsible stakeholder treatment and being a good corporate citizen.

The relevance of the moral character and integrity of the manager, the third topic, is considered in Chapter 6 through a discussion of some key moral competencies for leading business firms. These include the fundamental competencies of willingness to serve, and practical wisdom. There are other competencies which make the former operative, and these are related to relationability, fortitude and moderation.

This book, exploratory in character, will hopefully be useful to managers, executives, consultants and business students. Academics of management may also find suggestions for discussion and further development.

Domènec Melé
Barcelona, 30 June 2011

CHAPTER 1

WHY GOOD MANAGEMENT REQUIRES ETHICS

Management in industry at the present time has the blood of a new youth coursing through its veins. It is full of a new vigour and a new enthusiasm. Its practice is being overhauled, both from the scientific and from the ethical points of view.[1]

OLIVER SHELDON (1894–1951), Chief Executive Officer and a writer on management in the 1920s

The author of these words was the CEO of Rowntree's, a family business based in York, UK, whose activity was centered on confectionery.[2] In Sheldon's time, Rowntree's was a growing company. He successfully restructured it and adopted a more functional style and professional culture.

Along with his managerial activity, Sheldon wrote a book entitled *The Philosophy of Management*, which is a small gem of early management thought. Contrary to other influential thinkers of his age, he held that good management was much more than technique. It also encompassed concern for people and ethics.

In Sheldon's view, good management should provide decent working conditions and should consult with employees and involve them in decision-making in the workplace. He thought that industry existed for more than the profit of shareholders. Service to the community was the primary motive and fundamental basis of industry.[3]

Management has been defined in a very simple but comprehensive way as "the art of getting things done through people". According to Peter F. Drucker, "management is the specific and distinguishing organ of any and all organizations".[4]

Understanding management in its broadest sense, it can be said that this activity has been exercised since ancient times.[5] However, modern management thought began in the late 19th century. The

1

manager's task is to promote effective and efficient cooperation in order to achieve common goals in organizations. However, this is not all. Management is a human, not mechanical activity. It is carried out both by people and for people – conscious and free beings – and this involves ethics.

One very simple and intuitive approach to *ethics* is to consider the service or damage to those people who receive the effects of a human action. Another way is to pay attention to what is generally considered personal moral qualities. Integrity, trustworthiness, courage, sense of service, and their antonyms, are examples of these. Although ethics is actually much more complex than this simple outline, this introduction may be sufficient for the purpose of this chapter. We will try to explain ethics more extensively in the next chapter.

Here we will firstly discuss how ethics, in a positive or negative sense, are intrinsic to management. For this purpose, we will begin by analyzing the dynamism of the manager's action, including the effects on both the agent (manager) and the recipients of the action, and its subsequent consequences. We will argue that ethics are embedded in management in three different ways: (1) through managerial decisions, (2) through the ideas and values (ethos) which drive the practice of management and (3) through the manager's moral character. We will then consider the favorable consequences that ethics has in management, and finally we will discuss why good management requires ethics.

THE MANAGER'S ACTION AND ITS DYNAMISM

In order to understand why ethics is an essential part of good management, it is necessary to consider the manager's action and its dynamism, that is, the effects of such action and the subsequent consequences for future actions. At this point it is important to escape from the narrow view of managerial action focused exclusively on efficiency and economic results and to consider the whole picture of the manager's action, including its effects and the response of those who in one way or another are recipients of that action (Figure 1.1).

As with any human action, the manager's action has effects which are both external and internal for the agent (the manager, in our particular study).

External effects

A manager's decision and subsequent action bring about three different types of external effect:

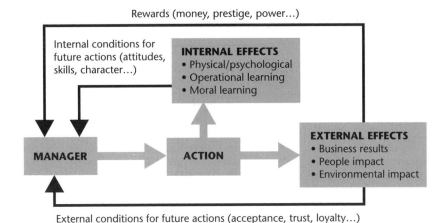

FIGURE 1.1 **Dynamism of the manager's action**

■ *Material or business results*, achieved in pursuance of a certain aim associated with the action. These results can be measured in economic terms by considering the sales income and expenses in developing, producing and selling a product and, consequently, its profitability. The number of sales, the purchasing of the product by different groups of people, and the market share are other possible measures related to business results. In more general terms, material results express the *effectiveness* of achieving a goal and *efficiency* in the use of resources.

■ *People impact.* Satisfying people's needs and desires comes before business results. The latter are a consequence of offering what people want. A first impact on people is *satisfaction* or dissatisfaction with the product and how it is sold. Buyers will also acquire *learning* through the purchase process (treatment received, reliability of the sales-person, accuracy of the information provided, and so on). The people impact may even be wider than this. Let us consider, for instance, the case of an educational product with innovative software. Apart from satisfaction caused, the product will probably have a certain impact on the student learning process. In addition, some people may get a job promoting and selling this product. The whole picture of a manager's action considers that the immediate external effects can bring about *further effects* or consequences. Thus, the introduction of this product may have consequences for the educational climate, or may spur a journalist to write an article for or against, or may spark a certain reaction from consumer associations if the supposed educational purpose is doubted.

■ *Environmental impact.* The manufacturing of the product can generate waste and pollution. In the case considered, packaging of the educational software, and the product itself, especially its disposal, may also have certain impacts on the natural environment.

Internal effects

Taking a decision and performing an action also brings about internal effects for the agent, and these effects can generate learning which will influence future actions. Three internal effects can be distinguished:

■ *Psychological and physical effects*. Actions can have both emotional and physical effects, expressed in terms of satisfaction or dissatisfaction, anger, joy, anguish, fatigue, nervous tension and so on. These effects will be remembered by the agent and create certain *attitudes* which will influence his or her subsequent actions. Taking into account his or her emotional experience, the manager will foresee if a certain action would cause satisfaction or other psychological or physical effects, and this can be motivation to perform or not perform similar actions in the future. With the previous example, the manager who introduced the educational software product may have experienced difficulties in promoting it, but also satisfaction from the positive response of customers and from the results achieved.
■ *Operational learning*. Agents learn by acting and this learning may be applied in subsequent similar actions. The learning includes acquiring *practical experience* and *technical skills*, a greater ease in performing similar actions and in interacting with people like those the agent has already dealt with. The manager can learn how to sell the product, which arguments are more convincing, how to judge the proclivities and tastes of the buyer and so on. Operational learning, therefore, increases managerial skills acquired by acting.
■ *Moral learning*. The agent has a greater or lesser awareness of how an action serves or damages people and this causes a certain impact on the agent, encouraging a certain disposition to act in the same way in future actions. Being aware that the product is sold with fairness, without deception or fraud and makes a positive contribution to education generates a good moral conscience and a disposition to similar good behavior in the future. Justice, honesty and a sense of responsibility are some stable dispositions (*moral habits*) that can be acquired by acting. Courage and self-mastery exercised through the action also bring about the corresponding dispositions in the agent, shaping his or her moral quality. These dispositions will be present in future actions.

Dynamism of the action effects

Both external and internal effects have an influence on the agent. External effects have repercussions on the agent, firstly from business results. They provide rewards in different ways, including money, prestige, power and so on. In contrast, these effects may also be negative. The impact on people and the environment has repercussions for the agent, too. People receive the action impact and learn whether or not it is favorable to their interests. They also perceive the moral quality of the action and evaluate the integrity and honesty of the agent. As a consequence, they respond to the agent in favorable or unfavorable terms, praising or recommending the product, being predisposed to buy other products of the same brand and so on, or the contrary. Environmental impact can also be evident, either directly or through people for or against a managerial action. In summary, the reactions of people and, to some extent, that of the environment, provide conditions, favorable or otherwise, for future managerial actions.

Internal effects, as noted, have an influence on managerial attitudes, skills and in the development of the moral quality of the manager. Internal effects are cumulative and in each situation the manager – like any other human being – is endowed with the internal effects of his or her previous actions. Managers have skills and experience acquired through their actions and certain moral habits, good or bad, also acquired through their deliberate and free actions. Thus, there are managers with great integrity and others with less. In a certain sense, each manager is a result of his or her biography, being made up of a great number of deliberate and free actions.

ETHICS IN THE MANAGER'S DECISIONS

We can find ethics as an intrinsic element of the manager's decisions, and consequent actions, by considering that (1) managers, in being rational and free agents, have the capacity to experience responsibility and bear it, and (2) human actions involve morality, since they affect people and the environment for good or bad.

Responsibility inherent in any deliberate and free decision

Moral responsibility is a key concept in ethics, and a generally shared experience. This means being answerable for one's own decisions regarding good or bad. We may well agree that "most people, most of the time, take, or want to take, responsibility for the effects of their decision and the corresponding actions on others".[6] Ethics presupposes the capacity to make decisions and to act in one way or another or even to refrain from a certain course of action.

The manager's actions are, first of all, human actions, carried out with deliberation and freedom. Like any human adult with sound mental health, managers are capable of reflecting on their actions, on the situation in which they find themselves and the foreseeable consequences of such actions. They form intentions about how they will act and, what is more, they experience that their actions are their own, that is, they proceed from their own freedom; and consequently they are aware that they should answer for what they have decided and done. Being the author of his or her own actions, the manager bears the responsibility inherent in any human action.

Societies, too, from very ancient times have held that people – including managers – are responsible for their actions, although such responsibility can be attenuated or fully excused by certain cognitive, psychological or social factors. This is the basis on which people deserve praise or blame for what they do and the justification for penal codes.

There are vast studies on *legal responsibility*, including that of managers, which develop the idea that managers bear certain responsibilities in accordance with the law. But beyond legal responsibility derived from legal duties, managers bear moral responsibility for their actions derived from the above-mentioned human capability of reflecting on one's own actions and their consequences, and being aware of how these affect people. In some cases, legal duties are quite narrow and compliance with legal duties does not absolve managers from moral responsibility.

One example can make this clear.[7] John Manville was, up until the 1980s, the worldwide leader in the asbestos sector, a product which has multiple and significant applications in a number of industries. Unfortunately, the fibers of asbestos come off in the production process and handling during its installation can lead to serious disease if particles are inhaled, including lung cancer after several years of latency. For a number of years legislation was quite lax, relatively high levels of fiber concentration in the air were accepted, while medical research produced increasing evidence of how dangerous asbestos was for human health. The company could have reduced risks by investing in safer processes and by taking other measures to protect the workers' health, but it did nothing. After a number of lawsuits the company was held culpable and managers were found guilty, for they knew or should have known the danger of its star product, especially as they were the worldwide leader in asbestos.

In contrast with legal responsibility, moral responsibility is not only related to wrongdoing but to any kind of action. Most managerial actions entail very positive effects for people and for the manager him or herself. Being aware of this positive impact helps us to understand that ethics are about more than avoiding wrong: primarily, ethics are about doing good.

Morality intrinsically associated with human decisions

Managerial decisions and the corresponding actions entail morality, that is, they have a certain quality related to right or good conduct. For a long time, the fashion was to say that "business is business" or "the business of business is business", expressing the amorality of business and, consequently, of business management. Today, few people would publicly maintain such a position, although some might think it. We remember many managerial actions or omissions which one could scarcely term amoral: well-known corporate frauds, the adulteration of foods, deception in disclosing financial information, factories which exploit workers and show a lack of respect for human rights, the lack of safety in mining, the depletion of natural resources and the scandalous pollution in some countries, disasters such as Bhopal in India or Chernobyl in the former USSR, to mention just a few.

Fairness in obtaining economic results is one aspect of the morality of the managerial action, but so too are the human, social and environmental impacts of such action, which can be evaluated in ethical terms. Morality in the context of managerial decisions does not only have a negative application. Most managerial actions actually show positive morality for their contribution to people's wellbeing and to the common good of the firm and society (see pp. 116–125).

The moral evaluation of a decision requires further development, which will be provided in Chapter 3 (see pp. 45–71). But it is worth noting here that morality is intrinsic to managerial action, and not an extrinsic addition. The description of the morality applied is required for an accurate description of a fact, although morality often remains implicit, especially for actions which entail a real service to another. In other words, business facts are not "value-free", as some people may believe. Take, for example, Bernard L. Madoff, founder and chairman of a Wall Street investment securities firm (Bernard L. Madoff Investment Securities LLC). In 2009, he received the maximum sentence of 150 years in federal prison for a massive fraud of about $65 billion involving thousands of investors. The fraud began in the 1990s, or even before, and consisted in paying returns to investors of his firm, not from any actual profit earned by the organization, but from money paid by subsequent investors. This "technique" is known as a "Ponzi scheme". At a certain point everything was discovered and he could pay no more. A full description of Madoff's action is not that he operated a Ponzi scheme, but that *he committed a fraud by using a Ponzi scheme*. Both the moral and the technical elements are integral parts of a unique action.

ETHICS IN THE MANAGERIAL ETHOS

In its early days management was seen as an extremely formal activity. The scientific management of Frederick W. Taylor[8] with its accurate planning of tasks and procedures was paradigmatic. Similarly formal was the approach of Henri Fayol.[9] However, within a few decades, and without rejecting these formal aspects, managerial thought and managerial practice began to stress the importance in management of the existence of an informal organization underlying the formal structures. Informal organization includes the richness of the human condition, within which are a variety of motivations and types of relationship. A comprehensive position was offered by the Harvard professor John Kotter, who highlighted the importance of both maintaining formal and ordered organization and dealing informally with people. He exemplified the extent of informal organization by showing how seemingly wasteful activities like chatting in hallways and having impromptu meetings are, in fact, quite efficient.[10]

Management entails an ethos

From a different perspective, today it is widely recognized that management is a varied and often complex activity where *art, craft* and *science* meet. Henry Mintzberg,[11] who emphasized these three drivers, affirmed that some managers tend to lean one way or another, in accordance with their own personal preferences: toward creative art, practical craft, or organized science, although in his view an appropriate balance is necessary.[12] It should be added that underlying art, craft and science there is a certain ethos which drives how management is understood; it is the "philosophy" of management adopted.

- *Art* draws on intuition, creativity, imagination, acting with flexibility in specific situations, developing unique alternatives, novel ideas to solve an organization's problems. It is the vision to foresee opportunities and threats, anticipating how the organization and its environment will be, and foreseeing the turbulent twists and turns of organizational life.
- *Craft* is consolidated experience and action-based learning. Craft requires time, action and reflection on success and errors in perform-

ing managerial functions. It can also be developed by considering the best practices in management, learning from case studies, taking advice from experienced and expert managers.

- *Science* provides valuable information for managers. It includes correlations in empirical business data, market and marketing research, structure of the markets, financial reporting, hypotheses on cause–effect relations in certain problems, statistical figures and economic information, along with psychological and sociological studies. Above all, science supplies analytical tools, models and theories.

- *Ethos* is at the core of the art, craft and science of management. The word *ethos* comes from ancient Greek, with the original meaning of "custom, disposition, habit". Currently, ethos is understood as the "distinctive spirit" of a practice, institution or social organization; and also as fundamental values peculiar to a specific person, people, culture or movement. Applied to management, ethos refers to how management is conceived. More precisely, ethos could be defined as the driven ideas and values in the practice of management. For instance, a management ethos can be based on uprightness and integrity. This ethos contrasts with others, such as a management understood in Machiavellian terms, using cunning and duplicity in a manager's conduct in order to retain power or achieve business interests. Ethos is particularly important for the purposes of this chapter.

Art, craft and science can have a reciprocal influence and ethos, whatever this may be, occurs in management by shaping art, craft and science, as noted. At the same time, the way in which art is practiced, the experience accumulated and the findings of science can lead the person to a re-think of beliefs and values and to a change of ethos. Thus, we should consider not three but four interrelated elements, although the fourth, ethos, has a guiding role for the others (Figure 1.2 overleaf shows these drivers of management without their mutual interrelation).

Ideologies can have a significant influence in shaping a particular ethos in management. Thus, a certain ethos can encourage management selfishness and investor short-sightedness. This is a different ethos to that which encourages a sense of responsibility and concern for others, and awareness of sustainability in terms of *profits*, the *planet* (natural environment) and *people* (the triple "P"). Similarly, accepting the idea that "the business of business is business" brings about an art exclusively concerned with economic results. This "art", which considers individuals as mere resources for gains, has a different focus to others which see business as a human activity which can serve or damage people, and people not only as resources but as individuals with human dignity and innate rights. This latter way of understanding carefully considers

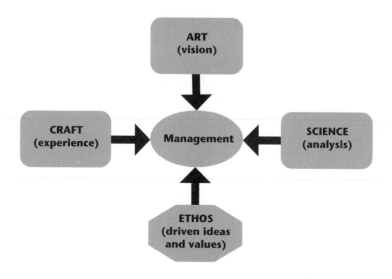

FIGURE 1.2 **Aspects of management**

human, social and environmental impacts of management practice. Similarly, accumulated experience is also related to the guiding principles in learning. Ethos meets science, too. Social sciences, such as economics, sociology and psychology, which are widely used in management, are conditioned by the hypotheses and *models of man*, business and society which are applied by the specific practitioner.[13]

National or organizational cultures, wisdom traditions and religions can also make a contribution shaping a certain ethos in management. In this sense, in the 1980s, Japanese management, or the art of Japanese management,[14] became popular. Nowadays, it is generally accepted that there is a particular leadership and management style in China[15] in which Confucianism, Daoism and other Chinese philosophies have an influence.

In addition, in each company there is usually a certain "management philosophy" which can have a decisive influence on how management is exercised. This ethos can derive from the ideas and values of the founder and/or subsequent leaders and from the culture generated within organizations. A particular management ethos has been embedded for a long time in organizations such as Johnson & Johnson, IBM, Merck and HP, to mention just a few.

Scrutiny of managerial ethos

Ethos entails a certain view or model of the human being, as well as an idea of the business firm and the purpose and responsibilities of

10

business in society. Management can be exercised, for instance, considering that a person is only a self-interested individual, or thinking that he or she is also capable of disinterested generosity. Likewise, management practice can assume that the business firm is a mere aggregate of individuals united through a nexus of contracts, or a complex human community. Similarly, wealth creation can be taken as the exclusive purpose of business in society.

Alternatively one might add that businesses should also contribute to society through other ends inherent in their business activity. Related to this, one can assume that the only responsibility of managers is to strive to maximize shareholder value, or, on the contrary, that managers bear responsibility for all stakeholders, not only for shareholders. All of these approaches can be evaluated through ethics. (We will return to this topic in considering the purpose of the business firm in society: see pp. 109–114.)

Ethics are not only a reference in *evaluating the management ethos*. Ethics can *inform the managerial ethos*. The consideration of ethics can also lead to the *development of a new ethos*, which can inspire new models and practices of management and leadership. This is, for instance, the case in values-based management in companies where culture and management have been influenced by the values of their founders and subsequent leaders.

ETHICS IN THE MANAGER'S MORAL CHARACTER

Ethics are also present in the manager's moral character. Managerial actions denote such character and, in turn, help to shape it. Actions can show honesty, diligence, concern for people, a great sense of service, or the very opposite. Greed could be the great motivator of giant corporate frauds such as those performed by some former executives of Enron, WordCom, Parmalat and Adelphia Communications, among many others; not to mention those who abetted the subprime crisis in 2008. In striking contrast we see a fair number of executives with behavior characterized by professional will and humility who were part of those companies studied by Jim Collins which went from *good to great*.[16] Professional will and humility are personal moral qualities embedded in the manager's character.

At this point it is worth distinguishing between personality and character. *Personality*, a term taken from psychology, denotes the totality of qualities and traits which are peculiar to a specific person, but not all the traits of a person are morally relevant. This is the case of having a disposition to practice a sport, or of having a preference for rye bread. The term *character* is typically used to refer to the particularly moral dimension of a person.[17] Thus, it can be said that *character*, or with greater precision *moral character*, is a part of personality related to moral quality.

The importance of moral character in management is emphasized when one considers that a person with a good moral character displays good behavior with naturalness, ease and enjoyment. A generous person performs acts of generosity easily and with full naturalness, without a great effort, and enjoys acting in such a way. An egoistic individual, on the other hand, if he or she carries out an act of generosity will do so without spontaneity, with reluctance, and by making a considerable effort.

Being generous, honest or diligent are *stable good dispositions* of the character, or in short good moral habits, what traditionally are called *virtues*. Contrasting with virtues, vices are bad stable dispositions of the character; bad moral habits. Egoism is taken as a vice, contrary to generosity, and dishonesty and laziness are vices which contrast with the virtues mentioned above.

Virtues give an inner strength for good behavior, and their exercise makes one more virtuous. A person with very strong virtues may not require a code of ethical norms, but for less virtuous people, good behavior can be aided by following ethical principles and norms, by asking wise people for guidance, and by reflecting on practical wisdom (see pp. 40–42 and 135–137) accumulated over time.

Moral actions are inextricably linked with moral personal qualities. *Codes of conduct* can help to foster good behavior, but their mechanical application is not sufficient for acting ethically at all times and in all situations. This requires good moral character; virtues.

HOW ETHICS CONTRIBUTE TO GOOD MANAGEMENT

Ethics are therefore embedded in management through managerial decisions, through the ideas and values (ethos) which shape how managerial practice is understood, and through the manager's moral character. But can these three elements contribute to good management? What consequences might they produce? We try to analyze these issues next, pointing out seven consequences of ethics in management (see Figure 1.3).

(1) Humanizing business

As noted, management focuses on doing things effectively and efficiently, but through people. Management would not be good on

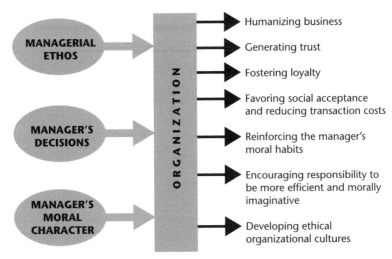

FIGURE 1.3 **Causes and consequences of ethics in management**

the whole if efficiency was achieved at the cost of inhuman working conditions or if people acted at the marketplace like animals in the jungle.

Managers should promote efficiency, but not at any cost. Ethics remind us that people in an organization are rational and free beings, and not cogs in a machine, and they require respect and treatment in accordance with the human condition.

In the face of a mechanistic view of management which was quite common in the early 20th century, Oliver Sheldon, the business executive we highlighted at the beginning of this chapter, wrote as early as the 1920s: "Industry is not a machine; it is a complex form of human association: The true reading of its past and the present is in terms of human beings – their thoughts, aims and ideals – not in terms of systems and machinery. The true understanding of industry is to understand the thoughts of those engaged in it."[18] This is a type of ethos which contributes to the humanizing of business.

Humanizing business is a long journey. The primitive mechanistic view of management was progressively substituted by another in which people were considered as individuals who can be motivated in order to increase their efficiency. This meant a more human approach but the full humanity of the person was still not considered. A truly ethical ethos should do this.

Ethics go beyond good treatment of people purely for the sake of increasing efficiency, and consequently economic results. Obviously, this does not exclude a greater efficiency coming as a consequence of dealing with people ethically. But ethics is valuable in itself and not only as an instrument for profits. Ethics leads to the appreciation of and respect for people, every single person, not as a mere resource for economic goals but for their humanity (see pp. 30–31 and Chapter 4, pp. 73–100). In this sense, ethics gives guidelines for humanizing business.

(2) Generating trust

Ethics also contributes to good management in generating trust. Few would doubt the importance of trust in business. Both popular business books and serious academic research proclaim the necessity of trust in promoting interpersonal collaboration, effectiveness in teams, organizational development, successful and high-performance organizations, individual credibility, workable inter-organizational alliances, networks, the development of effective safety cultures within high-risk environments and other aspects of organizational life. Trust has also an influence on reducing transaction costs[19], as we will discuss below (see p. 16).

Trust is a subjective perception which, firstly, refers to persons who for some reason inspire confidence and, secondly, can also be felt for an institution or organization. Trust emerges when one comes to depend on the other's behavior and assumes that the latter, who could act in a way damaging to the former, will not do so, but act in a beneficial way. Trust entails, therefore, a situation of willing vulnerability of one (trustor) in respect of another (trustee). For instance, in supplier–buyer relationships, the buyer trusts the seller when receiving a product to enter into a contract without deception. In return, the supplier trusts that the buyer will pay following agreed conditions.

In a study widely cited,[20] it is argued that the formation of trust is strongly influenced by three principal factors of perceived trustworthiness – ability, benevolence and integrity. They applied these trustworthiness dimensions to interpersonal, intergroup or inter-organizational levels of analysis. As the authors of this study explained, ability refers to technical skills, competencies and characteristics in some specific domain. Thus, the recognized ability of a surgeon generates trust in patients who need a surgical operation. Similarly, it occurs with a general manager who is going to be hired. One can trust in his or her experience of managing another company successfully. When ability exists in some technical area, a person can trust that tasks related to that area will be carried out with an appropriate level of competence. Trustworthiness in ability is specific, since one can be trustworthy in one area but not in another. The other two dimensions are related to ethical behavior learned in previous interactions or in the perception of moral qualities of an individual, group or institution. Benevolence is the extent to which a trustee is believed to want to do good to the trustor aside from an egocentric profit motive. Benevolence is shown, for instance, in a mentor who wants to help the protégé, even though the mentor is not required to be helpful and there is no extrinsic reward. Integrity refers to the trustor's perception that the trustee adheres to a set of principles that the trustor finds acceptable; for instance, keeping one's word, honoring contracts and not telling lies.

Trust being a psychological state of the trustor, trust can be built on a flawed perception of reality. After Madoff committed the above-mentioned fraud (see pp. 7–8), one broker taken in by him mused: there was "something about this person, pedigree, and reputation that inspired trust".[21] However, trying to build trust on image alone is not durable. Sooner or later the truth will emerge and the consequences can be dramatic. When trust is lost it is not easily recovered.

Ethics lead to acting with benevolence and integrity and to promoting these qualities within the organization, beyond subjective perceptions. But when there is true benevolence and integrity, behaviors will be credible and the corresponding perception will be likely to adjust to reality better than if there is only an appearance of such qualities.

(3) Promoting loyalty

It is well-known how important it is for growth and profit sustainability to achieve long-term relationships with customers. To this end companies develop special programs giving inducements, they take care of their customers and even use personal gestures to show their appreciation to customers. Empirical research shows that when customers believe that the firm is ethical, the inducements and special treatment received are seen in a positive light and can help develop loyalty. Findings revealed that a salesperson's ethical behavior leads to higher customer satisfaction, trust and loyalty to the company that the salesperson represents.[22]

Organizations having *loyal employees*, who identify with the organization and are committed to it, are generally also highly appreciated. Loyal employees are willing to remain with the organization, make sacrifices for the good of the company and go the extra mile whenever necessary. Thus, loyalty has been qualified as the hidden force behind growth, profits and lasting values within organizations.[23]

Employee loyalty can be motivated by utilitarian or emotional considerations, but can also relate directly to the perceived loyalty and ethical behavior of corporate management. This is particularly true in the negative sense, when unfair treatment is perceived by employees.

Employee loyalty may also be inspired by managerial concerns over employees' interests and being supportive of employees' work, which can also be related to ethics. In the 1990s, for instance, downsizing, rightsizing and re-engineering with massive lay-offs, particularly in the USA, might not be perceived as ethically correct. This brought about a decline in employee loyalty, trust, morale, satisfaction and commitment.[24]

(4) Favoring social acceptance and reducing transaction costs

People who are the recipients of the manager's action and others who can in some way influence future managerial actions might react in different ways: accepting and even praising the action, showing indifference, rejecting or even presenting hostile attitudes which can make future interactions with the manager difficult, and at the extreme impossible. This will be the case with the stakeholders of a firm if we consider actions of the top management. Although, in some cases, *social acceptance* may not be connected with ethical practices, generally the contrary occurs. A lack of respect for people and for the environment, fraud and commercial deceptions lead to rejection and even hostile reactions against the guilty company, while most demonstrations of social responsibility are welcomed and contribute to a company's reputation.

Suffering a lack of social acceptance is a precarious position to be in, even more so when managerial action has been illegal. Lawsuits and their penalties and losing managerial or corporate reputation can occasion serious damage to managers and to their companies.

A usual ethical behavior also has an influence on transactions. In any transaction there is an agreement between two or more parties in terms of exchange. Transactions do not take place in a vacuum. Contracts reinforced by laws, social regulations and customs, shared norms within a community, control and trust in the counterpart contribute to a sense of security in the fulfillment of contracts and in the enforcement of behaviors. The lower the trust, the greater the transaction costs in terms of costly contracts and measures of control.

Dealing with people with moral integrity and good reputation provides a sound foundation from which transactions can take place. Such behavior generates trust, and a minimum of trust, be it in institutions, corporations or personal behaviors, is always necessary.

Furthermore, transactions involve costs, which include the energy and effort it requires to find the proper conditions, contracts and subsequent control to avoid opportunistic behaviors, which seek self-interest at any cost. These costs increase in environments with scarce ethics, because more resources are necessary to avoid unfair behaviors. In marked contrast, in environments in which there are high ethical standards and people with integrity the transaction costs tend to be lower. The less integrity a person has, the lower the trust and the greater the transaction costs.

(5) Reinforcing the manager's moral habits

As noted (see p. 4) when considering the dynamism of the action, the agent in acting experiences a *moral learning*, in the sense of developing a certain disposition to act in the same way in future actions. Thus, the manager reinforces his or her moral habits – virtues or vices – through the action.

Similarly, as he or she acquires or develops skills through the action, moral habits are acquired. This reality, to which we do not always pay sufficient attention, was realized by Aristotle more than 2,400 years ago. "For the things we have to learn before we can do them, we learn by doing them, e.g., men become builders by building, lyre-players by playing the lyre; and so too become just by doing just acts, temperate by doing temperate acts, brave by doing brave acts."[25]

In contrast, when a manager decides to accept a shady deal or to act unfairly, he or she will be disposed to repeat similar actions in the future, starting what can become a snowball effect. An energetic reaction against wrong behavior is necessary to recover good dispositions.

(6) Encouraging responsibility to be more efficient and morally imaginative

Efficiency basically depends on technical competencies but concern with being efficient is not alien to ethics. Efficiency can bring about wellbeing for people and a better livelihood, which is not out of the ethical scope of care for people. Such considerations provide moral motives which encourage responsibility to develop competencies to be more efficient and to seek the most appropriate means to increase efficiency.

A truly moral manager is not simply a kind soul, unconcerned about efficiency and profitability, and who is even less negligent or careless in managing business, and a person who sees obtaining business results as an important aspect of his or her moral responsibility. Efficiency, as has been said, should not be obtained at the price of violating human dignity or through inhuman means, but in harmony with this, and a manager should seek the best possible results.

In addition, moral managers will not avoid situations in which acting ethically seems incompatible with making profits. They think of other options and seek alternative courses of action in which they can harmonize ethics and efficiency or profits. Obviously, this is not always possible, but often is. This is what some authors call *moral imagination*: "Moral imagination enables one to assess a situation, evaluate the present and new possibilities, and create decisions that are not narrowly embedded in a restricted context or confined by a certain point of view".[26]

Being morally imaginative is not only for solving dilemmas by trying to avoid misbehavior and being efficient, but also to find innovative solutions to meet human needs. A paradigm in seeking innovative solutions which combine ethics and efficiency is the well-known micro-credits system (small loans to poor people possessing no collateral) introduced by Muhammad Yunus,[27] which made loans accessible to people with no possibility of gaining access to conventional credit.

In ordinary business, moral managers may also be aware of human problems, for instance in reconciling family and work life. Their moral concern may lead them to seek solutions in which ethics and efficiency come together.

(7) Developing ethical organizational cultures

Explained in a very simple way, *organizational cultures* are deep, shared convictions and values and common practices and behaviors within an organization. Organizational culture has an influence on people involved in the organization, in the way they interact with each other and with people outside the organization.

Today it is generally accepted that certain organizational cultures have the potential to generate sustained competitive advantages. This is most probably the case for ethical organizational cultures due to the effects of ethical behavior on trust and loyalty.

Creating trust-based organizations requires the building of trust through leadership, but also through organizational architecture and organizational culture.[28] The moral character and behavior of leaders has a major impact on trust, but the formal and informal aspects of the organization promote or erode trust over time. Organizational culture is important for building trust.

Among the factors which influence an organizational culture, the following are often mentioned: the corporate mission and values, the control system employed, organizational and power structures, and some practices such as corporate symbols, rituals and routines, stories and myths. Apart from these there is another which is really crucial:

leadership.[29] All of these are related to managerial ethos, managerial actions and practices and the manager's character; elements all related to ethics, as has been discussed above.

Although organizational culture is a very elusive concept to measure, the values and moral character of founders and managers who have led a company over time are likely to have great weight in building up ethical organizational cultures. In any case, we feel comfortable in affirming that ethics contribute to good management in developing ethical organizational cultures, too.

WHY GOOD MANAGEMENT REQUIRES ETHICS

To conclude we will discuss why good management requires ethics. If ethics contribute to good management, it seems desirable to include ethics in management. However, ethics are not only desirable, but necessary for truly good management.

Setting ethics principles and standards apart from management produces not only inhuman management but also bad management. Kennett R. Andrews, who was a celebrated professor at Harvard Business School, argued that ethical failures are management problems too. Companies that are successful over time build their success on creativity and energy, but also on the will and commitment of their members; and "such commitment cannot be sustained by strategic decisions that are ethically unsound".[30] Andrews also suggested that executives can ask for advice, but ultimately they must make a decision, relying on their own judgments to settle infinitely debatable issues. That is why the character of the decision maker is decisive, especially in making decisions where there are no clear choices or absolute answers. Consequently, "inquiring into character should therefore be part of all executive selection – as well as all executive development within the corporation".[31]

In practice, the language of virtues is not a stranger in many managers' language. Listening to what managers themselves say when discussing excellent managers and their behaviors, it has been reported that "virtue language" is fluently used by practicing managers. Such language is important to understanding managerial excellence, if being virtuous is an aspect of being a good manager. This means following the Golden Rule ("treat others as you would like to be treated"), being one who "walks the walk", rejecting gossip and showing a willingness to accept responsibility for one's actions and decisions. As a study shows, managers' language includes virtue terms such as genuineness, humility, trustworthiness, loyalty, fairness and courtesy.[32]

In addition, we must remember that organizations require cooperation to achieve their goals; and managers are essential to foster cooperative and coordinated work. Managerial misbehaviors can affect cooperation, since such conduct decreases trust and loyalty, and erodes authority.

Lack of ethics in management can also affect employees' motivation. At this point we might remember that beyond the common goals of the organization, those who form it can have different motives for cooperating toward such goals. Moral managers can foster a sense of responsibility and moral commitment to employees. First of all by steering clear of negative moral motivation due to managers' misbehaviors (e.g. disloyalty toward workers can be followed by another disloyalty) or of certain structural conditions which make acting for moral motives difficult, or that may even stimulate bad conduct (this is what often happens in bribery). Secondly, by acting as positive *role models* (displaying personal moral qualities), managing the organization with an ethical ethos, taking moral decisions and practicing management in such a way that can motivate workers' good behavior.

One can argue that immoral managers get good results. Maybe, but this is not all, as noted. Furthermore, managers who leave aside ethics, seeking only efficiency, may get short-term results, but trust, loyalty and culture will suffer. Consequently, long-term results can be jeopardized.

Is ethics actually possible in real management?

Last, but not least, one frequent objection should be considered. This refers to ethics in the real business world. Some might say: "Ethics are nice when everything is going well, but unrealistic in a strong competitive environment or in a system in which managers are pressured into getting profits, and often short-term profits."

There is no doubt that there are managers who may experience serious difficulties in acting ethically where they are under strong external pressures. This can be the case in corrupt environments where it could be difficult to get a contract without paying a bribe to politicians or civil servants; or to get additional income without hidden fraud when the bottom line is red; or in situations where there is a lack of financial capability to pay for raw materials or commodities, and the manager believes that lying to the supplier can avoid the risk of having to stop production.

Besides the examples above, managers may also feel a certain internal impulse to act unfairly when an ethical behavior can seem opposed to personal economic gain or ambitions of power. For instance, strong economic incentives depending on short-term profits can lead managers to avoid necessary investments for the long-term or to sell assets which can put the future of the company at risk. Immoderate ambition for power or success, or foreseeing difficulties for one's own career, can lead managers to collaborate in unfair actions or take wrong decisions in order to please their boss. Thinking of abandoning the company soon, an unscrupulous manager might adopt opportunist behavior (see pp. 90 and 154) at the cost of damaging the organization and passing this problem to his or her successor.

Nobody would say that acting ethically – with integrity – is always an easy task. Sometimes it is difficult to make a sound ethical judgment about whether a certain course of action is ethically right or wrong, but the most difficult thing may not be this, but having sufficient courage to do the right thing; and this depends on the moral character of the manager, on his or her integrity. Both rational and religious motivation can foster acting with courage and integrity.

Ethical management may be difficult but it is not impossible. In some situations, there may be no other way than acting with courage, even at the cost of sacrificing personal gain, career or business success, if a manager wants to maintain his or her personal integrity and not corrupt him or herself as a human being. However, in many other situations, the manager will use *moral imagination* (see p. 17) to solve the problem and look for an alternative which is both ethical and efficient. Maybe the problem of a bribe can be solved by reporting it to international agencies, changing the red bottom line requires going to the causes and acting on them, and a negotiation with the supplier can bring about an appropriate solution. In any case, acting without ethics can be astute and cunning management, but it is not good management.

EXECUTIVE SUMMARY

Analyzing the manager's actions is fundamental to understanding why ethics contributes to good management. Two types of effects can be distinguished in these actions: external to the manager and internal. External effects entail business results which have repercussions for the manager in terms of money, power, prestige or other rewards, and also an impact on people and occasionally the environment. The latter bring about learning in people and a certain reaction, which can be of acceptance, indifference or rejection. This conditions future actions in terms of trust or mistrust, loyalty, and so on. Internal effects to the manager origin attitudes, practical experience and technical skills and moral habits, which also influence future actions.

Ethics consider human action, the service or damage people receive in acting, and also personal moral qualities. Ethics are embedded in management, firstly through decision-making, which entails responsibility and morality. Secondly, through ideas and values (ethos) which drive the practice of management. A third way in which ethics are present in management is through the manager, the agent of management, and his or her moral character shaped by good or bad stable dispositions (virtues or vices), which support his or her actions and behavior.

Taking ethical decisions and implementing them, managing with an ethical ethos and being a moral manager contribute to good management by (1) humanizing business, (2) generating trust, (3) fostering loyalty, (4) favoring social acceptance and reducing transaction costs, (5) reinforcing the manager's moral habits, (6) encouraging responsibility to be more efficient and morally imaginative, and (7) developing ethical organizational cultures.

In fact, ethics are not only desirable for their contribution to management, but necessary for truly good management. Ethical failures are management problems, and ethical achievements are managerial achievements. Moral managers can foster cooperation and promote the moral motivation of employees beyond money and other extrinsic motives.

Ethical management can be difficult in some situations which require great courage, but it is not impossible. In many cases, the manager will use imagination to solve the problem, looking for an alternative course of action which is both ethical and efficient.

CHAPTER 2

BASIC ETHICS FOR GOOD MANAGEMENT

... if you are not always asking yourself if what you are doing is good, you slip.[1]

FRANÇOIS MICHELIN (b. 1926)
French businessman

François Michelin led the Michelin group from 1955 to 1999. This group manufactures and sells tyres for all kinds of vehicles in more than 170 countries, and accounts for 70 per cent of the replacement tyre market. A grandson of Michelin's founders, François had a "business philosophy" inherited, in part, from his family. François' vision was that every human being is unique and unrepeatable and deserves great respect and care. Considering the incomparable dignity of being a person, he stressed the importance of the individual treatment of workers, listening to them and to their deepest motivations, giving them the opportunity to develop talents inside and outside the plant. He emphasized that people have all the means to better themselves or to destroy themselves,[2] and believed that work gives each person not only an occasion to do things, but also to grow themselves as human beings. Although no company is perfect, Michelin has generally sought to apply this philosophy. This approach is probably not unconnected to the invention of the radial tyre, which became a crucial technological innovation. It was due to Marius Mignol, a Michelin employee who had joined the company as a typist in the printing department. Within the company, Mignol's creativity and talent were appreciated and he was promoted to technical functions where his invention prospered.

François Michelin's beliefs are a practical way of understanding ethics. He believed firstly that every human action performed with deliberation and freedom has an ethical content; and secondly, recognizing

23

the human dignity of every individual, he believed that people, by acting, grow themselves as human beings.

In Chapter 1 we introduced ethics in a very elemental way. Now we discuss some basic ethics in more depth, beginning with a short discussion of what contributes to good behavior.

WHAT CONTRIBUTES TO GOOD BEHAVIOR

According to the renowned psychologist James Rest,[3] moral behavior is determined by four interrelated psychological components which contribute to moral behavior as well as decision-making. These are: (1) moral sensibility; (2) moral judgment; (3) moral motivation; (4) moral implementation skills or moral character (Figure 2.1). These components must be developed for a person to be morally mature and correct.[4]

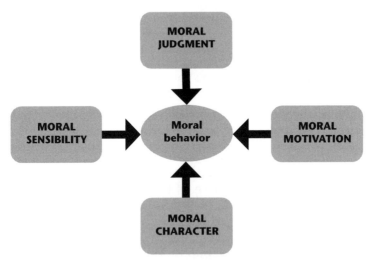

FIGURE 2.1   **Psychological components of moral behavior**

Moral sensibility

This refers to the recognition of the moral aspects of a given situation, or the moral issues implied in a given proposal, or to the awareness of the moral dimension of a certain decision. Such sensibility can be expressed as understanding how a decision or an action can affect people's physical and emotional wellbeing. Moral sensibility also covers the recognition of moral principles and guidelines which frame

the moral dimension of a situation or an action, and can give awareness that some ethical norm may have been violated.

Managers could demonstrate moral sensibility, for instance, by
being aware that a task assigned might result in negative consequences
for the health of those involved in the task. A lack of moral sensibility
may lead managers to not see and take into account the full consequences of and responsibilities for their actions, and act less carefully
than they otherwise would.

Managers with scarce moral sensibility tend to see each problem only
in economic terms, or act by considering only their personal or corporate
interests. In contrast, managers with moral sensibility are always asking
themselves if what they are doing is good, as François Michelin suggests.

Moral judgment

This refers to the evaluation of whether a human action or a decision
is good or bad. It is triggered by moral sensibility, which leads to a
judgment about the acceptability of an action from a moral viewpoint
or to deliberation over the most appropriate course of action from this
perspective. Making a sound moral judgment may be very easy in some
situations, while in others it can be very complex. Several elements
are relevant in considering ethics in decision-making (see pp. 56–66),
including some basic ethical principles and values, such as those we
consider below.

Moral motivation

This is the driving force of the will to decide to act or not to act for
moral reasons. Moral judgment acts on the motivation providing the
immediate motives for accepting or rejecting an action. While moral
judgment states "this is the right thing to do", moral motivation drives
one to do it: "I ought to do it". Deeper motives behind moral judgment
come from the desire to maintain personal integrity and to act virtu-
ously. Religious motives can reinforce moral motivation, and in some
individuals these motives can be extremely important.

Moral motivation occurs with other types of motivations. There is
no problem if moral motivation is consistent with these other types.
However, moral motivation can also conflict with motivations based on
useful rewards derived from the action (money, power, status, prestige),
or with those caused by the pleasure or learning that the agent can obtain
in performing the action. Here appears the temptation to subordinate
the moral motives to others such as money, power, pleasure and so on.

When one of these latter motives becomes the dominant motive for acting, there is no prospect of moral or good behavior, only of wrong-doing or misbehavior.

Moral character

This is shaped by virtues, as noted in Chapter 1 (see pp. 11–12), and is built by acting with moral motivation and by doing good. Moral character provides inner strength for good behavior and helps when there is tension between moral motivation and other motivations. Virtuous people – people with a strong moral character – tend to have more moral sensibility than others who are less virtuous.

GAINING AN UNDERSTANDING OF ETHICS

Ethics provide a rational foundation to spontaneous morality. At first glance this might appear simple, but diverse and often sophisticated theories of ethics have been proposed throughout the past 2500 years and these can cause a certain confusion. Our approach will avoid complex philosophical discussions by presenting an approach based on very basic concepts which are easily understandable.

For Ancient Greek philosophers, pioneers of ethical thought, the study of ethics looks at the kind of person we are and how we can grow as human beings. They believed that the moral traits of character – virtues – give those who possess them the propensity to act in ways that promote human flourishing. Plato and Aristotle discussed in great detail virtues such as justice, friendship, temperance (moderation) and courage.[5] Virtues, which are central to these thinkers, are recognized as expressions of human excellence, and they are believed to give us the inner strength to achieve the highest human good.

According to Aristotle, ethics are a practical matter. We ask what is good for human beings because we want to know how to live a fully human life, and how to flourish. Motives for human action are called goods by Aristotle. We can easily agree on a number of these (to be healthy, enjoy justice and friendship, experience pleasure, make money) but not all of them bring about human flourishing. Some goods, such as money, are instrumental for other goods. In contrast with these *instrumental goods* there are *intrinsic goods* which are wanted for themselves. Among these latter goods which are sought for their own sake alone, we can distinguish two types: *pleasant goods* (for example, enjoying food or being honored) and *moral* or *human goods*. Moral goods are not only wanted for themselves for this psychological satisfaction, but for their intrinsic contribution in growing as human beings (for example, justice, friendship). The latter are absolute goods, and are often called simply *goods*.

Over time, and especially from the 18th century onward, the understanding of ethics turned to focus on principles, norms and duties rather than on virtues. Its aim, associated with Modernity, was to show what a right action is and to solve ethical dilemmas by applying principles and other tools for moral reasoning. Thus, two main streams of thought emerged, one based on duties (*Deontologism*), of which the outstanding representative is Emmanuel Kant.[6] The second is founded on the principle "the greater happiness for the greater number", which requires an arithmetical calculation of the consequences of an action, generally evaluating in terms of utility or satisfaction (*Utilitarianism*). Jeremy Bentham and John Stuart Mill[7] are the main proponents of this latter approach.

In the late 19th and early 20th centuries some authors, facing these formal ethical systems based on abstract principles without specific content, focused on non-formal *ethics of values*. According to Max Scheler,[8] one of the main proponents of this school of thought, ethical values are objective and universal; they do not change. It is our perception of values that really changes. In different cultures and historical periods some values are emphasized while others are ignored. In spite of this, many common values can be found in the main religions and traditional wisdoms worldwide. In a certain sense, the concept of ethical values substitutes for two other related concepts which were central in Ancient Greece: good and virtue.

It was only in the late 20th century that the importance of virtues in ethics was recovered. This does not mean that we should abandon principles, duties and norms, which are also crucial elements of ethics. Goods (and implicitly virtues) and duties are actually considered in some wide definitions of ethics. Thus, Merriam-Webster's (Word Central) Dictionary defines ethics as "a branch of philosophy dealing with what is good and bad and with moral duty and obligation".[9]

The recovery of virtue makes sense, since values and virtues are *not* interchangeable terms. Although ethical values and virtues are related, there is a substantial difference between the two notions. Values refer to what is considered worthy, while virtues refer to traits of character. It is clear that laziness is not a good habit and that it is possible to look favorably on a hard working person, even if they do not possess the corresponding virtues. In other words, values are related to the mindset of the person, while virtues refer to personal moral qualities of character.

The notion of ethical values is more related to the classical notion of human good. Ethical values come from considering human goods as *motives* for acting. Because human goods are intrinsically worthy, they become motives for good behavior. Justice, honesty, generosity, kindness, courage, moderation and so on, are expressions of human flourishing, therefore "human goods", and are also "ethical values" or ethical motives for acting.

After this exploration, we will present some basic ethical principles, which are taken as self-evident, although some people can have more difficulty than others in discovering these, hampered by insufficient moral disposition or experience of life.

These ethical principles are different from *personal values*, which are subjective, and *social values*, which are part of a cultural context. Personal and social values may or may not be in agreement with ethical values. In this sense, Stephen R. Covey rightly distinguishes between principles related to truths (human goods) and "subjective values". He does so through a brilliant example: "A gang of thieves can share values, but they are in violation of the fundamental principles we're talking about."[10]

BASIC ETHICAL PRINCIPLES

The Golden Rule

A very basic ethical principle, mentioned in Chapter 1, is the "Golden Rule". As noted (p. 19), the Golden Rule can be explained in simple terms as: "Do not do to others what you would not want done to you", but also in positive terms: "Treat others as you would like to be treated". A more accurate expression of this could be:

> Treat others only as you would be willing to be treated in an identical situation.

The Golden Rule was formulated by people belonging to different cultures to promote good behavior and also as a way to resolve conflicts. With different formulations but with the same essence, the Golden Rule can be found in Ancient Egyptian society, Zoroastrianism, several Greek philosophers, Judaism, Christianity, Islam, Hinduism, Jainism, Confucianism, Taoism, Buddhism and Secular Humanism, among other religions and traditional wisdoms. Nowadays, neuroscience tells us that this universal principle is registered in the human brain.[11]

The global extension of the Golden Rule, more than likely without any cultural influence from one community imposing it on another, shows the capacity of human rationality to discover so basic a principle of morality as this, which permits people to live together in a harmonious and peaceful way. Although the way in which one applies the Golden Rule can depend on the context and situation, its very basic prescription remains a permanent and universal principle of ethics, as an expression of unchanging justice (see pp. 33–36 and 137–138).

The Golden Rule provides a basis for the modern concept of human rights, since the Golden Rule is reciprocity in human interaction, in such a way that everyone has the right to be treated as one would require for him or herself. The Golden Rule is included into the first principle of the Natural Moral Law, which we will discuss next.

The First Principle of the Natural Moral Law

Human goods, and the corresponding ethical values, are rooted in human nature, and therefore are universal, inasmuch as all people share the human condition. Human goods are known intuitively and can be understood through people's behaviors. Both good and bad behaviors show what a human good is. As Covey pointed out, the self-evidence of human goods is grasped by considering the absurdity of a life based on their opposites.[12] Being a victim of injustice or egoism, or feeling oneself deceived or hated helps us to understand that justice is a human good. There are widely shared ethical values, including justice, generosity, honesty, a sense of service, generosity, courage, moderation, compassion, care, benevolence and others. Human goods are discovered by one's conscience as a calling to act in accordance with these, so they entail a sense of obligation. They lead to what is known as the First Principle of the Natural Moral Law, which is classically framed as follows:

> Good is to be done and pursued and evil to be avoided.

In other words this can be expressed as:

> Seek truly ethical values and act in accordance with them.

This expresses the moral calling to flourish as a human being. Although this principle may seem very vague, if we consider the goods mentioned above, plus others which can easily be grasped rationally from our natural inclinations, it is in fact an elemental principle. It permits the development of an ethic based on human nature, and so is trans-cultural and common to all people. Some precepts derived from the first principle of the Natural Moral Law are made explicit in the Ten Commandments, a set of basic ethical norms, which, with some small differences, are common to the three great monotheistic religions: Judaism, Christianity and Islam.

Another possible way to make this first principle more practical is to consider the intrinsic worth of every human being, and the subsequent recognition and respect of human dignity as a crucial human good.

Human Dignity and the Personalistic Principle

The recognition of and respect for the dignity of every human is generally considered a crucial way of doing good. Human dignity expresses the idea that every human individual is intrinsically worthy, and therefore each person deserves respect and great consideration.

Human dignity, according to some thinkers, is rationally evidenced. Kant held that persons have not merely a relative worth, that is a price, but an inner worth – dignity. Consequently, persons should be treated as an end, never merely as a means. In other words, people cannot only be considered as simply means to obtain certain ends. Workers, in a certain sense, are human resources within an organization, but never *mere* resources (see a development of this point in pp. 80–87). They are people, endowed with dignity. Having a wider scope than Kant's approach, the Principle of Human Dignity or Personalistic Principle has been formulated in these words:

> No human being should ever be treated as mere means to an end.
> On the contrary, persons should be treated with respect and also with care and benevolence.[13]

Human dignity is not situational but constitutive, that is, intrinsic to the human being. In other words, every human individual is endowed with *constitutive dignity*, whatever his or her circumstances might be. Such dignity differs from another meaning of dignity, which is context dependent, and called *situational dignity*. This refers to the worth that one acquires in exercising his or her position in society (e.g. being a good doctor) or the "dignity" inherent in a position with authority (ruler, judge, etc.). In this sense, the dignity one has can be lost through misbehavior or by acting improperly (e.g. committing a crime).

Human dignity can be traced back through Judeo–Christian tradition. Human beings were created in the image and likeness of God and so God bestowed them with an intrinsic worth (*constitutive dignity*). Such dignity is accepted worldwide by a vast number of people, although it is sometimes expressed in different terms. Thus, in Confucian teachings, the term "dignity" is reserved to indicate worth that one acquires by behaving properly within relationships (*situational dignity*). But the analysis of concrete practical cases from a Confucian perspective suggests that it is possible to devise courses of action that honor both situational and constitutive dignity.[14]

The recognition of the dignity of every human being and treatment in accordance with this is also included in the Preamble of the *UN Universal Declaration of Human Rights*, which affirms "the dignity and worth of the human person and the equal rights of men and women". This means that every human being has an intrinsic value, regardless of race, age, sex or any other particular condition and also independent of any legal recognition (or lack thereof). Respect for human dignity requires dealing with each person with respect, and even with an attitude of care and benevolence. Respect for human dignity, along with the Golden Rule (see p. 29), provides a solid base for human rights. In a certain sense, any human right is rooted in human dignity.

Although some argue that the validity of human rights cannot be derived from any first principles, others hold, in our view correctly, that the validity of human rights is human dignity. In turn, human rights, which have become operative through a great number of legal instruments, provide for the protection of human dignity.

The recognition and respect for human dignity entails rules which involve great consideration for human beings, including workers, consumers, suppliers and so on. They should never be manipulated, that is, used through insidious or deceitful means for one's own advantage. Nor can people be considered or treated as objects or property, or used for selfish purposes.

Principle of the Common Good

The Golden Rule and the Personalistic Principle focus primarily on interaction between individuals but in a wider sense both principles can be extended to groups of persons which also deserve respect and consideration.

Humans are relational and social beings (see pp. 79–80) who live in society and, in practice, belong to several communities (family, neighborhood, local community, business, church, nation and so on). Underlying this fact, there is what is termed *sociability*, a crucial human characteristic (see pp. 79–80) which expresses the natural inclination for living together and the rational understanding that living together in a friendly and peaceful way, cooperating within the common needs of one's own community, is a basic human good.

The concept of the *common good* refers to shared goods within a community: the fruit of the contribution of those who form such a community. All those who are part of that society in some way share these common goods. Thus, the common good is more than the sum of individual interests within a community. With regard to society at large, one can identify respect for human rights, enjoying clean air, living in peace, sharing social cohesion and good systems of education and health care as aspects of the common good, to mention just a few. Within a business firm, the common good is found, for instance, in having good products to sell, a solid financial situation, a good work climate with a strong sense of cooperation and care, mutual trust and fairness, concern and respect for the environment, and a sustainable position. The common good includes all external conditions which contribute to the human flourishing of individuals and their respective communities.

The Principle of the Common Good can be formulated as follows:

> People, individuals and social groups within a community should contribute to the common good of their community in accordance with the capacities of each and should sacrifice individual interests when these conflict with the common good.

People within business organizations have common goals and numerous and complex links; they are a community which is part of a larger community. Working for the common good for mutual profit within a community is what this principle requires; and this includes within business organizations. Managers, employees, shareholders, customers and other stakeholders can have different interests, but these should all be harmonized and even subordinated whenever necessary for the common good of the firm as a whole. Maintaining the competitiveness and sustainability of the firm (see pp. 115–116) over time and respect for human dignity and rights are important considerations to which individual interest should be subordinated.

The First Principle of the Natural Moral Law is central. The other principles, which provide complementary aspects, are consistent with this.

BASIC ETHICAL VALUES AND VIRTUES

Ethical values and virtues are intertwined with ethical principles, and particularly with the First Principle of the Natural Moral Law (see p. 29). Ethical values (human goods) included within this principle bring about corresponding virtues, acquired when one acts in accordance with such values. Thus, doing good is not only beneficial for others and for a good society, but also for the agent. The person who performs an action in accordance with ethical values becomes a better person, with a higher level of virtue.

Virtues are therefore related to the above-mentioned First Principle of the Natural Moral Law, since this prescribes acts which develop virtues. In this way we find mutual interdependence and harmony

32

between human goods (ethical values), norms (duties) derived from these goods and virtues (moral character)[15] (see Figure 2.2).

Explained in more detail, the knowledge of human goods (ethical values), entails a certain imperative (norms, duties) to act consistently with these goods; and acting in accordance with ethical norms generates virtues. In turn, the virtues make the knowledge of the human goods easy.[16] An "honest person" (a virtue) easily recognizes "honesty" (a human good), which requires "acting with honesty" (a norm or duty); and acting in accordance with ethical norms (e.g., honesty) reinforces being a virtuous person (an honest person).

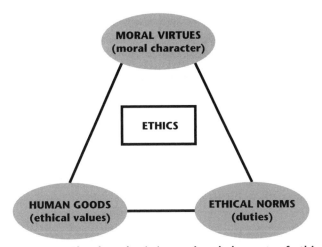

FIGURE 2.2 **The three basic interrelated elements of ethics**

That being said, it may be worth remarking on some ethical values and the corresponding virtues. We will consider three, which in a certain sense, cover many others: justice, truthfulness and intelligent love.

Justice

Living together in a friendly and peaceful way is a crucial human good, which requires justice. Justice leads us to give to each other what is due, that is to say our rights. As with other ethical values, justice can be seen as an ethical value (a human good), a duty or a norm for action and as a virtue.

Justice is widely recognized in both antiquity and our own times. The prophets of the people of Israel railed strongly against injustice, specifically against the oppression of the weak and needy by the powerful. Time has shown that justice is a precondition for peace.

The Greek philosophers lent great importance to justice, too. They saw justice as a rational requirement of human affairs, something necessary to harmonize relations with others and essential for social cohesion and order. Justice was seen as "the force of reason" which is to be preferred to "by reason of force" in seeking social harmony. The importance of justice for harmony was especially highlighted by Socrates and Plato. Aristotle, who also shared this high opinion of it, felt it was a fundamental virtue and principle for life in society. Without justice it would be difficult to have harmony in relationships and social peace in any community or institution, including business firms.

Modern thought has fixed above all on that aspect of justice which involves *redistribution*. This is especially so in the political context where justice is taken as the guiding principle for public institutions. Many influential authors have adopted a focus more akin to the ideological than the ethical when dealing with the concept, Thomas Hobbes being a case in point with his view that justice was an authoritative command of the State. From this perspective, by definition, the other side of the coin is that what the law prohibits is injustice. Others, following *Contractualism*, see justice as derived from the mutual agreement of everyone concerned, and understand distributive justice as an impartial distribution of goods (justice as fairness).[17] In contrast, for *Utilitarianism*, public institutions are just when they manage to maximize aggregated utility.

Beyond ideological and cultural differences in understanding the scope of justice, it must be remembered that justice is an ethical category, which leans toward giving to each his or her due. This means that justice seeks to give reasons for what is right, beyond simply that something is prescribed in law. It seeks to identify what rights each person or social group has. Justice, then, is opposed to the abuse of power and to the exploitation of the needs of others.

Justice demands respect for people and for their rights, as these are rights they have through the mere fact of being a person (human rights), or because they are rights granted by some other condition, be this a contract or a state concession.

There are various forms of justice which can be usefully considered here, even if this is only at a very elemental level.

General justice

This refers to the obligation to respect others and to give to the community that which it is due. Included here are the rights of the person (the right to life, to good reputation, to the truth, to a dignified life, to religious freedom, etc.), and that which is necessary for the common good of the community. In a firm, the respect for these rights is present in a variety of situations: health and safety in the workplace, just evaluation of the person and his or her work, respect for the reputation of others, not revealing defects and faults unless it is truly required, avoiding negative criticism and so on. General justice is sometimes termed *legal justice*, because it includes compliance with just laws (those which are not contrary to human rights and other ethical demands), which specify the obligations that must be met. As long as a law – backed by the legitimate authority – specifies general obligations of justice, there is a moral obligation to follow them.

Commutative justice

Commutative justice relates to justice in exchanges. In these, justice seeks to adjust – to equal – relations following arithmetic proportions. It indicates that each party in the exchange should have an equal value. In the context of a firm, buying and selling are typical situations which demand commutative justice. This throws up the well-known argument about *value measuring*. Each party to a transaction may have a different perception of the value of the good to be traded, but in a free market the price agreed or the accepted valuation of trusted third parties can bring the matter to a just conclusion. In contrast, in exchanges where one party is much more powerful than the other, and the latter is in a situation of need, the person enjoying the power advantage must be especially sensitive to the demands of commutative justice. In the case of *monopolies*, the regulation of *monopolistic practices* is often in force to prevent abuse of power.

Distributive justice

This refers to the sharing or distribution of positions and benefits within a community. Here the *adjustment* must follow a certain proportion, which comes from equitable criteria which may make provision for the contribution made to the community and for the personal merits or needs of the members of the community. Problems of distributive justice can be found within a firm, both in what is *advantageous* (position, remuneration, distribution of bonuses, etc.), and what is *onerous* (unpopular shifts, downsizing of workforce, etc.). Distributive justice is in opposition to *favoritism* and *egalitarianism*, both of which, in different ways, fail to take account of real merits or contributions.

Restorative justice

Restorative or *reparative justice* refers to the obligation of repairing the harm caused by a previous action, or to the restitution which is due to compensate for an injustice committed (for example, the return of something stolen, the restoration of reputation after an unjust accusation, etc.). In a certain way, this form of justice is a particular type of commutative justice.

In the organizational context, restorative justice focuses on repairing indiscipline or offences caused by misconduct; and also on compensating the harm caused by misbehavior. This is the case of the manager who applies sanctions in incidences of indiscipline or offences which erode the common good of the firm. *Penalization* should be both proportionate and effective in satisfying the superior good of justice and in correcting the offender. It can never be motivated by hatred or a desire for revenge.

Truthfulness

Along with justice another crucial ethical value is truthfulness. Every human being wants to know the truth. Nobody likes to be deceived and lying is generally considered ethically wrong. The conduct of those who seek the truth, tell the truth and act in accordance with the truth is generally appreciated.

Truthfulness, or veracity, refers to the habitual observance of truth in speech or statement and in behavior. Truthfulness requires respect for the facts and making statements which correspond to the actual state of affairs, as far as they can be known. Truthfulness also entails a permanent disposition to search for the truth and to act accordingly.

Truthfulness is necessary for social life and, without it, trusting one another is not possible. People who lie or act deceitfully are considered unreliable.

Truthfulness requires, first of all, the avoidance of *lying*, that is, expressing a falsehood with the intention of deceiving in speech or action. Lying is condemned for its very nature, because it perverts the communication of thought and feelings which involves the expectation of knowing the truth. Moreover, lying often leads to damage to third parties by distorting the knowledge of the truth to which they may have a right.

There are other ways of deceiving contrary to truthfulness, in which there is not a blatant lie. *Deceiving* takes place, for instance, in making an indirect, ambiguous, or contradictory statement, minimizing or downplaying aspects of the truth, or hiding relevant information.

Certain exaggerations can also result in deception and even edge toward a lie (e.g., in advertising, "this car is the best sold in its class", when it is not). However, depending on the context, certain instances of exaggeration or *hyperbole* – exaggeration to create emphasis or effect – can hardly be expected to deceive recipients of the message (e.g., again in advertising, "you will be happier with this car"; "Smile. Coke adds life"). Often the aim here is to convince the counterparty of the strong credentials that the product or service possesses, when the credentials are in fact weak or totally non-existent.

Deceiving is unfair when people expect not to be misled, but there are sports and games in which deceit is a part of the rules of the game or deception is consented to in advance by the players. This is also the case with *bluffing*. Intimidation with a false display of confidence may not be seen as immoral when it takes place in the context of a game. Notice, however, that the context of a game is a very particular situation, and not the universal norm. In business, practical wisdom should determine the appropriate way of acting in particularly tough situations, e.g., in a negotiation process, without lying and also respecting your counterpart's rights, and avoiding naïve behavior.

Lack of truthfulness can be present in business in different forms, one of which is *fraud* – an intentional deception made for personal gain or to damage someone. Lying and deceiving can also be found in personal or corporate communications, financial disclosure statements and auditing and reporting on a variety of matters. This may be done by blatant falsehoods, such as forgery of checks and invoices, but is more common through calculated ambiguities, by distortion of the reality or other forms of misrepresentation.

Truthfulness also requires disclosing information to those who have the right to know it. *Transparency* refers precisely to information disclosure, although this concept can have a wider meaning which includes openness, clear and complete information and accountability. Being transparent has, however, its limits. While lying is not allowed, no one has an obligation to reveal the truth to those who have no right to know it. Nor must everything that one knows be communicated indiscriminately; there are *legitimate secrets*, for instance, which should be kept. Respect for privacy, the good and safety of people or institutions and the common good are also motives for non-disclosure of information. Being silent ("no comment!") or using discreet language is not contrary to truthfulness in these cases. When an unjust aggressor tries to extract something from somebody, and silence or discreet language is not sufficient, an ambiguous or deceitful answer can even be acceptable. In a moral sense, this would be an act of *legitimate defense* rather than a lie.

Honoring one's word is also an important expression of truthfulness, which is extremely important in business, as is keeping promises.

Legitimate contracts – so essential for business life – require truthfulness in terms of *good faith* and sincerity in providing the relevant information, with no intention of deceiving the other party.

Intelligent love

Business has traditionally been based on contracts and duties of justice, and justice is probably the basic value in business, along with truthfulness. However, there are other relevant human values in dealing with people such as care for the other's legitimate interests, benevolence and selfless friendship. We group these within intelligent love, understood as love in its moral sense and driven by true knowledge of the real needs and legitimate interests of the other.

Love can have different meanings. One is based on feelings of attraction to and desires of possession of another. In classical Greek this love was termed *eros*. This type of love, based on attraction and often passionate, differs from the form of love which is understood as affection which seeks the true human good, even at the cost of personal sacrifice (*agape* in classical Greek).[18] The latter, intelligent love, is more a reflective love which seeks to know what is truly good for the other, even with self-sacrifice. Intelligent love entails a sense of affection toward others, but not irrational feelings or mere *sentimentalism*.

Two thinkers as dissimilar as Bertrand Russell, a famous British philosopher who declared himself an agnostic, and Pope Benedict XVI, although obviously from two different perspectives, agree on the importance of "intelligent" love. According to Russell,[19] a good life is one inspired by love and guided by knowledge; a knowledge in which science is particularly important. He believed that, although both love and knowledge are necessary, love is, in a certain sense, more fundamental, since it leads intelligent people to seek knowledge in order to find out how to benefit those one loves.

In a parallel manner, Benedict XVI proposed love guided by truth (*love in truth*) as a basic ethical principle, stating that "Charity [love] does not exclude knowledge, but rather requires, promotes, and animates it from within".[20] For him, knowledge of truth and love are inseparable.[21] Thus, Russell and Benedict concur that love should be moved by knowledge, but for Benedict knowledge is wider than that coming exclusively from experimental science, believing as he does that human intelligence is not confined to observable data alone.

Intelligent love entails *care*. Care means concern for people's needs, problems and *legitimate interests*. It is important to underline "legitimate", since interests which do not have a moral justification should be excluded from intelligent love. Otherwise, care will become sentimentalism.

Caring for others is closely related to the notion of *sympathy* (etymologically "feeling together"), an attitude by which one person stands with another with *compassion* (etymologically "suffering together"), meaning feeling pity for other people's needs. Compassion can be found in most religions and also in some modern moral philosophers. In the Bible there is repeated insistence on compassion in more than 90 texts. It is particularly eloquently shown in the *Parable of the Good Samaritan*,[22] in which a Samaritan, a stranger and enemy of the Jews, takes care of a Jewish traveler who was beaten, robbed and left half dead by the roadside. The teaching here is that concern for others is universal.

Buddhism holds compassion in very high consideration in its concern for alleviating suffering wherever it may appear. For Buddhism compassion isn't just a positive virtue, but an essential means – along with wisdom – for realizing enlightenment, the goal of Buddhism. Within this ancient wisdom, compassion is understood to mean active sympathy or a willingness to bear the pain of others.

Some modern thinkers have emphasized *care* from different perspectives,[23] presenting it as a responsibility and even as a necessity for organizations, arguing that care reinforces relations and networks. Some have even taken care as a central element of an ethical theory (the *ethics of care*).[24] There are valuable elements within this theory, such as safeguarding and promoting the specific interests of others involved in every situation one may be involved in, and paying especial attention to those who might be vulnerable to the consequences of any decision.

Intelligent love also entails *benevolence*. Understood not as an inclination to perform kindness but in its genuine and etymological meaning, benevolence – from the Latin *benevolence* (*bene*, well, and *volens*, wishing) – denotes a disposition to do good. It is also understood as friendliness and goodwill towards people, and very like neighborly love. Similarly, it is not unlike care and kindness, but goes far beyond these two values.

Benevolence, in its genuine sense, is generally considered as a human good, associated with the corresponding virtue "being benevolent" – or the habit of wishing well to persons – and with human flourishing. The existence of benevolence as an ethical value is made clear by a wide human consensus that those behaviors motivated by doing good to others are good, while a behavior which directly damages others for self-interest is seen as egoism. The latter carries a negative moral connotation, while the former is related to generosity, which is a virtue.

The great world religions and traditional wisdoms emphasize benevolence in different ways.[25] For their part, Ancient Greek philosophers emphasized justice above all, but did not forget benevolence – underlying justice they could have a motive of benevolence for human beings:

they "loved justice so because they loved their fellow men".[26] Aristotle considered benevolence in the context of friendship: "to a friend ... we ought to wish what is good for his sake".[27]

Intelligent love is not contrary to justice; rather, a truly intelligent love requires justice, since the disposition to do good entails, first of all, giving others what is due. But it goes beyond justice, and, as noted, it involves concern for other people's real needs, including what is necessary for human life and for developing as an individual.

Intelligent love provides a view of business emphasizing the inter-personal nature of human existence, beyond a mechanical exchange, and the human character of business relationships. In commerce, as in organizations, an intelligent love leads one to see the other as another "I", and to develop a deep appreciation of our common humanity. This sense of common humanity suggests going beyond the conventional reciprocity in business ("I give so that you may give") and intro-ducing a treatment with a sense of gratuitousness, which can be termed "friendship-based reciprocity" and a sense of "fraternal reciprocity".[28] Intelligent love is a driver for the highest levels of human quality in dealing with people (see pp. 85–87) and treating stakeholders not only with justice, but with a sense of proactive cooperation (see pp. 118–119).

THE NECESSITY OF PRACTICAL WISDOM

One practical problem is how to apply generic values in particular situations or how to solve cases in which two ethical values compete. Similar is the problem of applying universal ethical principles, such as the Golden Rule, the First Principle of the Natural Moral Law and the Principle of Human Dignity, in different cultures or in specific situations. These principles matter to everybody, everywhere because they are rooted in human nature, but they might seem too generic and of limited use for management. Of course they are generic, but they entail a set of minimum ethical requirements which can be easily identified. Thus, respect for human dignity implies, among other requirements, respect for human life, protecting health and never acting directly to damage people; and no slavery, exploitation or manipulation. It also prohibits mistreatment of persons or groups through insult, humili-ation, slander, blackmail or injury, it prohibits stealing and requires honoring one's word and telling the truth. These and other minimum requirements are frequently included in national and/or international legislation. These specific norms are more useful than generic principles.

However, minimum requirements are not everything in ethics. Furthermore, a tension exists between universal principles and particular situations. There may be instances of similarity between situations, but deep down each situation is unique. How can we apply universal principles, which obviously cover every situation, faced with the uniqueness of each situation? In situations of doubt and dilemma, one temptation is to adopt a *rigid universalism*, which rejects the particular circumstances of each situation and also excludes contemplation of consequences. Another approach is to opt for a relativism in which every moral judgment depends exclusively on the situation and the cultural context.

These extreme positions, which can be qualified respectively as naïve universalism and *crass relativism*, do not consider the human capability, called *practical reason*, which permits one to make sound moral judgments in specific situations. Practical reason is reinforced by practical wisdom, the virtue of good judgment, which can be cultivated and developed over time. These judgments are made in the light of universal principles, but also by considering both situational circumstances and foreseeable consequences.

Practical wisdom (also called *prudence* in a moral, non-utilitarian, sense) is the virtue of moral uprightness in making judgments. Aristotle defined practical wisdom as the "right reason in acting".[29] Practical wisdom, acquired through reflective practice and long experience, helps those who possess it to discern what is most convenient and suitable for each occasion in accordance with the human good.

The above-mentioned universal principles can be applied in different cultural contexts and situations due to their great comprehensiveness and flexibility. This is, for instance, the case in accepting gifts related to commercial transactions. Practical wisdom, when it has been cultivated, helps one to distinguish between an acceptable gift and a bribe. Practical wisdom will consider local customs, the value of the gifts and the context. Some rules can also help inexperienced people to solve this dilemma, but these rules – where possible – come from practical wisdom accumulated over time.

Practical wisdom also helps when making judgments in which two different values have to be balanced. For instance, communicating *inconvenient truths*, such as the possible non-renewal of a supplier's contract, must be done in a proper way. We need to tell the truth, without creating false expectations or giving unjustified praise to a product provided, but we also need to use kind words to emphasize positive aspects of the supplier's behavior and avoid any offence or devaluation of his or her self-esteem, as this would be showing a lack of respect for the human dignity of the supplier.

Exercising moral virtues also requires practical wisdom in order to know the *golden mean* between two irrational extremes. Thus, courage is neither cowardice nor recklessness. Practical wisdom helps one to determine the right behavior in each situation.

Practical wisdom concerns action, so it requires knowledge of particular facts even more than knowledge of general principles.[30] Practical wisdom requires maturation over time, acting with reflection and good sense, asking advice from suitable people, as well as learning from errors. Aristotle had no doubts in affirming that "whereas young people become accomplished in geometry and mathematics" (today we could add computers) "and wise within these limits, prudent young people do not seem to be found. The reason is that prudence is concerned with particulars as well as universals, and particulars become known from experience, but a young person lacks experience, since some considerable time is needed to produce it".[31]

EXECUTIVE SUMMARY

Moral behavior, understood as the moral aspect of behavior, is a common experience. Every language expresses morality in terms of good and bad, right and wrong, merit or blame, among others. Four interrelated psychological components converge in moral behavior: (1) moral sensibility; (2) moral judgment; (3) moral motivation; (4) moral character. Ethics provide guidelines for good behavior.

There are many theoretical approaches to ethics, which sometimes cause certain confusion. Within this variety, two main approaches can be distinguished. One is rooted in the Ancient Greek philosophers, pioneers in ethical reflection, who focused ethics on virtues and the human good. For them, the goal of ethics is being better as human beings (human flourishing). The second approach comes from Modernity, and focuses on principles, norms and duties, rather than on human good and virtues, which, to a great extent have been replaced by values. Its aim was to determine ethical issues and how to solve dilemmas. Principles and norms show what a right action is. This second approach has been the mainstream for the last two centuries, and continues to be important today. However, since the 1970s, virtues have been reconsidered and their importance and recognition is increasing.

Our approach here avoids complex philosophical discussions and presents an approach based on very basic principles, such as the Golden Rule and the Natural Moral Law, the First Principle of which states the obligation to act in accordance with that which can bring about human flourishing. The Natural Moral law is based on the common humanity of people, and on their rational capability to recognize a set of basic values and virtues and the moral imperative to act in accordance with these. Recognition and respect for human dignity, in which human rights are rooted, is another basic principle we propose, along with the

42

requirement to contribute to the common good of the communities to which one belongs, including society at large.

The chapter concluded by presenting three basic ethical values, and the corresponding virtues: justice, truthfulness and intelligent love. Justice renders to each his or her right, and it is expressed in different forms (general, commutative, distributive and restorative). Truthfulness refers to the habitual observance of truth in speech or statement and in behavior, and to a permanent disposition to search for the truth and to act accordingly. Justice, along with truthfulness, is the minimum ethical requirement in dealing with people, but it is not sufficient for fully ethical behavior. Intelligent love – understood as love driven by true knowledge of the real needs of the other – goes beyond this. Intelligent love entails, first of all, justice, but also care and benevolence, with a sense of gratuitousness within a framework of truly human relations.

Practical wisdom, the virtue of practical judgment, helps one to specify generic values and to make sound judgments when two different values have to be balanced. Practical wisdom is also essential in applying universal ethical principles in individual situations and in different cultural contexts. Last but not least, exercising moral virtues also requires practical wisdom in order to know the "golden mean" between two irrational extremes.

CHAPTER 3

ETHICS IN MANAGERIAL DECISION-MAKING

The values of a company's leader are evident in every strategic decision they make.[1]

KENNETH R. ANDREWS (1916–2005)
Professor at Harvard Business School for forty years

Kenneth R. Andrews was the Donald K. David Professor of Business Administration at Harvard Business School. He taught business policy and corporate strategy, and is considered one of the fathers of strategic management. He introduced the popular SWOT (Strengths, Weaknesses, Opportunities and Threats) method for evaluating business situations and strategic plans. He possessed both a business and a humanistic background. The latter came from his studies of American literature, which included a PhD on Mark Twain. He was editor of the *Harvard Business Review* between 1979 and 1985 and a fervent defender of ethics in management. In 1989 he edited *Ethics in Practice: Managing the Moral Corporation*,[2] made up of a number of articles on business ethics published in the above-mentioned journal.

Decision-making is generally understood as a process in which a problem is defined and, in order to solve it, the decision-maker seeks and selects a goal or set of objectives, from which a set of action alternatives are generated and evaluated, and finally one is chosen. A full decision-making process also includes the implementation of the chosen alternative and the follow-up and control of the results. If the results are not completely satisfactory a new cycle can commence.[3]

The above-mentioned book by K. R. Andrews includes several articles written by corporate leaders of companies such as Cadbury Schweppes, Standard Oil of Ohio, Phillips and Morgan Stanley, who reflect on tough managerial decisions involving ethical dilemmas, such as whether or not to divest operations in South Africa in the context of apartheid, how to handle a rogue division whose practices compromise the whole company, how to curb a slide into price-fixing in an overcrowded market. These are extreme situations, but ethics in managerial decision-making is not limited to those circumstances where the ethical content is particularly evident.

Neither is ethical decision-making only about dilemmas or a reduced number of issues. If ethics are a dimension of *every human decision* and action, ethics and the corresponding ethical judgment should be included in every decision. It is worth adding that decision-making is the core activity of managers at all levels of an organization. Depending on their position, managers will have to contribute to or make their own decisions on matters of *strategy*, *tactics* and *operations*. There are also small decisions to make on minor questions that crop up in the course of their daily work.

Some decisions are made quickly, but others take a long time. In business, decision-making commonly follows a process oriented towards solving a problem regarding something unsatisfactory or achieving an improvement.

If Andrews affirmed that the values of a company's leader are evident in every strategic decision, we can say that the values of the decision-maker are present in every decision he or she makes; and not only their values but also their virtues, which as noted previously are values internalized as traits of character.

Applying the values of a company's leader, generally the decision-maker, is obviously not a guarantee of making sound moral judgments, nor ultimately of making good ethical decisions. This would depend on whether or not such values are truly ethical values and also on the correctness of the ethical reflection on a particular situation.

In this respect it is worth pointing out that "ethics in managerial decision-making" can involve two different meanings. One is *descriptive*, based on behavioral studies, while the other is normative, and therefore *prescriptive*. While the former is about collecting and discussing empirical data in order to know what happens in practice, the latter deals with the rational understanding of the *managerial action*, and how ethics should be present in a holistic perspective of decision-making. This chapter focuses on the latter, and its aim is to give an understanding of how ethics can help managers to make sound moral judgments within the decision-making process. We will begin by considering the necessity of a holistic view in decision-making, by looking at the steps involved and distinguishing four different but interrelated dimensions in managerial decision-making, one of which is ethical.

A HOLISTIC VIEW OF DECISION-MAKING

Steps in the decision-making process

Often the decision-making process is presented as a set of steps, which with small variations includes:

1. *Formulation of the problem*. A problem emerges when a situation is not considered satisfactory and the decision-maker tries to solve it. Previous to the formulation of the problem and in preparation for the next steps, there is a gathering of data and maybe the advice of some experts or people who know the situation well.
2. *Outlining a goal and outcome*. These express what the decision-maker is trying to achieve, and that will presumably be a solution to the problem. It is the end of the decision.
3. *Generation of alternative courses of action*. This requires knowledge and experience but also imagination and creativity. Pooling ideas to develop alternatives could be necessary, especially with complex or difficult problems.
4. *Analysis and evaluation of alternatives*. First of all, an alternative should be viable, that is, effective as a means to achieve the goal and to solve the problem. Among several effective alternatives one might be more efficient than others in terms of use of resources and cost. Apart from these two criteria – effectiveness and efficiency – economics in character, other criteria should be considered, including ethical criteria, as we discuss below. The consideration of multi-criteria alternatives is particularly important in a holistic approach to decision-making.
5. *Election of one alternative*. A rational decision takes into consideration the analysis and evaluation of alternatives, including doing nothing, or a new alternative resulting from a combination of others. Finally one alternative is selected; and so the decision is made.
6. *Implementation of the action*. After the decision has been made, it has to be implemented in the right way and at the proper time.
7. *Evaluation of the outcome*. Monitoring and reflecting on the consequences of the action help to weigh up the appropriateness of the decision and to learn for subsequent decisions. This step can also involve making some modifications to minimize or avoid undesired secondary effects which were not considered when making the decision.

These seven steps can be summarized in three basic stages: *deliberation* (formulation of the problem, goal and outcome and, above all, generation, analysis and evaluation of alternatives); *decision* (election of one alternative) and *execution* (implementation and evaluation of the outcome).

47

Often the decision is presented as a deliberation in which pros and cons of each alternative are listed, followed by a progressive elimination of alternatives in which the decision-maker finds more cons than pros. This may be practical but it has the risk of seeing the decision-making process only in economic or utilitarian terms, and of reducing the whole of human rationality to instrumental rationality. This analysis of the decision in terms of costs and benefits – in some cases even reducing such analysis to the short-term – does not take into account a broader rationality which includes the morality of the action and the consequences of and learning done through the action.

Decision-making, if it is to be based on the big picture, should consider several relevant dimensions included in this process. Consequently, the analysis should be deeper than one based only on a list of pros and cons. We will return to this point, but first we discuss these relevant dimensions.

Decision-making: four interrelated dimensions

We have already considered the manager's action and its external and internal effects (see pp. 2–5). These effects can have consequences for the manager's relationships and for future actions. Thus, they should not be overlooked in decision-making; otherwise, we will not have a complete picture to enable us to make a good decision.

We can distinguish four aspects or dimensions in every managerial decision and its execution: the *instrumental, relational, internal* and *ethical*. The first three are related to the effects of the action or its subsequent consequences, while the fourth regards the ethical dimension of the action.

- The *instrumental dimension* refers to the business results sought in performing an action. These can be economic, technical or related to power, for instance. Two facets of the dimension relate to results, as noted (see p. 3): the *effectiveness* in achieving the desired results and the *efficiency* in the use of resources required to obtain such results.
- The *relational dimension* regards the future relations with the people affected by the action or, in a wider sense, relations with *stakeholders*, understanding those who are affected by the action or those who in some way can effect future actions by exercising certain influence on the decision-maker.
- The *internal dimension* refers to the learning produced by the internal effects of the decision and the subsequent action. This can include *psychological learning* regarding satisfaction or dissatisfaction with

the action, *operative learning* (skills) acquired as a result of the action and *moral learning* about the impact of the action on people and the environment, evaluated in terms of human good and ethical values. Moral learning develops or consolidates moral habits (virtues and vices).

■ The *ethical dimension* of the managerial action – as with any other human action – refers to the ethical evaluation of the alternatives by the decision-maker, and its influence on the intentionality of the agent in performing an action.

These four dimensions (see Figure 3.1) can have a certain dynamic interdependence, in the sense that one dimension can affect others in future decisions. Thus, focusing exclusively on the *instrumental dimension* (results) without paying attention to consequences of the action for future relations (relational dimension) would jeopardize the results of future actions (instrumental dimension). This is the case, for instance, of a manager who manipulates subordinates or co-workers and obtains excellent immediate results, but when those who have been manipulated realize this, they may react against him or her and even refuse to cooperate with the manager in the future.[4]

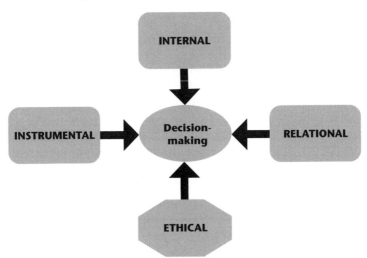

FIGURE 3.1 **Dimensions of decision-making**

The instrumental dimension can have an influence on the internal dimension, through fostering the learning of skills. The internal dimension also includes learning about the reactions of others who are affected by the action, and also certain learning about evaluating the internal states of those who are recipients of the action.

In turn, learning acquired (*internal dimension*) contributes to results (instrumental dimension) through skills, and the prediction of future reactions of the stakeholders (relational dimension). Moral learning, the other aspect of the internal dimension, fosters moral behavior in future interactions (see p. 17).

The *ethical dimension* of an action can have a positive or negative influence on the relational dimension, and through this it can influence the instrumental dimension, too. If a result has been obtained unethically, say by committing a fraud, probably the *relational dimension* will suffer, at least if the fraud is discovered. In contrast, the relational dimension can improve if the ethical dimension of the decision is good because of the consequences in terms of trust and loyalty. The ethical dimension can also have a direct influence on the instrumental. An example of this could be obtaining a contract due to one's ethical reputation and credibility.

Holistic approach and the primacy of ethics

As Herbert A. Simon[5] showed, humans have *bounded rationality*, meaning that humans are limited in their decision-making by limitations on information and time available, and by the information-processing ability of the mind. When faced with "maximizers" in the context of making a decision, that is, one who adopts a maximizing attitude in decision-making, Simon suggests being a "satisfier", or one who seeks to make decisions which are sufficiently satisfactory. This attitude leads to making *optimal decisions* in the current state of affairs, and also considers the long-term effects of the decision.

Holistic decision-making tries to make optimal decisions considering all relevant dimensions and using a multi-criteria approach. A seminal but interesting holistic decision-making approach was presented by Miguel A. Ariño et al.[6] They hold that holistic decision-making improves the quality of management, which leads to enhanced organizational quality, and firms with high organizational quality are more likely to survive, grow and be successful over the long term.

In the holistic approach presented here we suggest considering the four dimensions when analyzing alternative courses of action. This demands four different fundamental *evaluative criteria* (Table 3.1), and these can include other more specific references in accordance with each situation. Thus, relational criteria can consider current law and how law is applied in practice, the reaction of unions, whether unions are relevant, the current social values and sensibility to issues affected by a decision, and so on.

Dimension	Fundamental evaluative criteria
Instrumental	Cost–benefit analysis
Relational	Pros and cons for future relations
Internal	Development and degradation of internal capabilities
Ethical	Right and wrong; better and worse

TABLE 3.1   **Fundamental evaluative criteria for each basic dimension**

After evaluating an alternative we can find congruent evaluations, in which an alternative is in agreement or disagreement with all four criteria (e.g., with a new product to be launched which one presumes will be profitable, obtain good social acceptance, generate learning and be fully ethical). But we can also find conflicting evaluations, one or more being positive and another or others negative (e.g., a downsizing with a massive lay-off, which will make the firm more competitive and profitable, but may also damage workers and probably produce a bad social reaction from the employees, unions and public opinion, and demoralization in the remaining employees). Both situations posit dilemmas regarding which criterion is more important when choosing an alternative. In the former case, the question is what alternative should be selected as the optimal among a set of acceptable alternatives. In the latter, it is whether the decision (downsizing a company) is acceptable and in what conditions.

After analyzing and making the *evaluation of alternatives*, we may find that certain alternatives should be clearly rejected for one or more of the dimensions considered. Thus, an alternative might be unviable for economic reasons, for example, because it is not profitable or there is no way to get credit (instrumental dimension), it may be prohibited by law, or be legal but unwanted by the unions (relational dimension). In cases like these, where the learning is so negative that it jeopardizes the future of the organization (internal dimension), or the moral evaluation concludes that such an alternative is ethically unacceptable (ethical dimension). The rejection of one alternative, for whatever reason, leads us to focus on other alternatives.

A serious conflict can appear when an alternative is profitable but not ethical. The temptation here is to put ethics aside for the sake of economic results. But ethics regard human good and this entails an absolute priority over an interest, such as profitability, which is only an instrumental good; it is good for something, but not absolutely good (see p. 26).

After rejecting what is unacceptable for one reason or another – economically unviable or ethically forbidden –, the next question is to determine which of the alternatives is the optimal. Should economic rationality be the only criterion? Is the ethical criterion of doing good decisive without any further economic consideration? Here we have to take into account that in ethics there are negative and positive duties, and *moral responsibility* includes both types of duties. *Negative duties* derived from proscriptive ethical norms are acts that should never be performed, such as stealing, lying or accusing falsely (calumny). They signal certain universally minimum standards. In contrast, *positive duties* signal a direction and so have no upper limit. A person must do good to the limit of his or her abilities and resources available in any given situation. In contrast with negative duties, which generally are very precise, positive duties are not; they depend on the possibilities of doing good in each situation.

As noted above, ethics has primacy on economics, but further considerations are necessary. Even accepting this priority, what may seem ethically good in the short-term (avoiding lay-offs in a critical situation, for example) can become bad in the long-term (lack of competitiveness and maybe bankruptcy and greater loss of jobs). Thus, choosing the best alternative requires practical wisdom (see pp. 40–42) and weighing up both short-term and long-term effects in all their dimensions.

To select the best alternative, the decision-maker must also take the circumstances of each case into account, considering both economic feasibility (material means available) and social acceptance (resistance or encouragement to do what is right) which are clearly related to the long term. Thus, a business policy based on making short-term profits, which neither develops employee abilities (giving them repetitive and boring tasks) nor promotes good relations (showing a lack of kindness to workers with no attempt to develop a sense of service), even if not contrary to negative ethical duties, will probably be bad for results in the long term. We can conclude that all dimensions can have an important weight in determining the optimal alternative. In addition, we should consider that in managerial decision-making, the manager has resources and power to make decisions, but both resources and power are limited, and within such limitations he or she should decide, guided by the aim of doing as much good as possible in the given circumstances.

It is important to stress that in holistic decision-making, practical wisdom (or ethical prudence) plays a crucial role. It assists spontaneous ethical knowledge by providing practical knowledge of what is right to do here and now. Asking for advice from competent colleagues or experts, who in addition have a sense of integrity, may help to solve difficulties in conflicting evaluations or in choosing the optimal alternative from various acceptable options. We will return later to the role of practical wisdom in making moral judgments.

THE ROLE OF THE MANAGER'S MORAL CONSCIENCE

As noted before (see pp. 27–28 and 32–33), *ethics* is about virtues, principles and norms, and values, while *moral judgments* refer to the ethical evaluation of different alternative courses of action. However, sometimes people confuse both notions, for instance they talk about ethical disagreements when they mean that there is disagreement over moral judgments about particular issues, dilemmas or situations rather than over very basic ethical values and principles.

A well-known case can help to make the distinction between moral judgments and ethical principles and values clear. In 2011, following the earthquake and tsunami of 11 March, a dramatic accident occurred at the Fukushima nuclear power plant in Japan. This had serious consequences for the plant (it was forced to close) and, above all, for the people exposed to radiation. Tokyo Electric Power Co. (TEPCO), the company which operated the plant, admitted that it may have failed to accurately report cracks at its nuclear reactors in the late 1980s and 1990s. It is suspected that TEPCO falsified 29 cases of safety repair records. Previously, in 2002, TEPCO admitted to falsifying safety reports which led to all 17 of its boiling water reactors being shut down for inspection, including those at Fukushima.

In the Fukushima case, one can make a moral judgment on the morality on these fake reports, as well as on the responsibility of management and public authorities in this incident. One may suspect that Fukushima was a compound of negligence and natural disaster, but it could also be argued that what happened was completely unpredictable. It is not our purpose here to discuss this point, which would require much more information and a careful analysis. We seek only to distinguish between moral judgments and ethical principles and values.[7]

In this particular case, there are two ethical values at stake: truthfulness and justice. Truthfulness leads us to act with truth (principle of veracity) and justice to act with respect for other people's rights (principle of justice). Truthfulness requires us to avoid lies and to disclose due information (see pp. 36–37). Acting with disregard for human health, or not establishing appropriate conditions to protect it, is contrary to justice (see pp. 33 and 40). It would appear that TEPCO's managers failed to uphold either value.

It can be easy to make moral judgments in some cases, but less so in others. A sound moral judgment depends on the accuracy of the available information and on the rigorousness in making the judgment. Often, cultural elements or personal dispositions can influence moral judgment and bring conflicting viewpoints. Making sound moral judgments from solid ethical principles is a challenge; one which ethical theory helps us face.

Personal and corporate behaviors can be morally or legally evaluated from outside. Courts make such evaluations, taking the law as reference. People also make judgments based on ethical values and standards of morality. This is what happened with the TEPCO case. However, first of all, individuals – including managers – make, or should make, their own moral judgment within the decision-making process. These moral judgments are also known as *judgments of conscience* or simply *conscience*. This is the sense of the saying "my conscience does not allow me to take part in this business" or "my judgment is that this is a dirty business".

This chapter began by highlighting the sentence by Andrews that "the values of a company's leader are evident in every strategic decision they make". This is probably true for every decision, and not only for strategic decisions. But the question is, are one's own values correct and, above all, how do we make them practical in specific situations? Being aware of very basic values, such as justice and truthfulness, is not so very difficult. These and other ethical values are presented to our conscience and with a sense of duty (see pp. 32–33).

Following one's own moral conscience is a duty which demands the right of respect for personal conscience. This is generally a recognized human right, which gives support to conscientious objection by which a person refuses to do certain acts that are contrary to the imperatives of his or her conscience. However, the dignity of the person involves and demands rectitude of conscience. Following one's own conscience does not mean acting arbitrarily. Since each person has the ability to make his or her own moral judgments, he or she also has a responsibility to use all reasonable means to make correct judgments and to dispel any doubts that may arise.

At this point, it is important to remember the human ability for moral discernment and the corresponding moral intelligence or, in philosophical terms, "practical rationality", which differs from "instrumental rationality". When economists talk of rationality and rational behavior they generally refer to a specific form of rationality focusing on the most efficient or cost-effective means to achieve a specific end. This rationality is instrumental regarding a certain end and does not include any evaluative or ethical consideration. "Practical rationality", on the other hand, provides intellectual discernment between good and evil and permits us to make moral judgments.

Practical rationality formulates moral judgments regarding particular situations. It requires acquiring ethical knowledge and developing practical wisdom (Figure 3.2):

- *Ethical knowledge* provides fundamental guidelines for making moral judgments. It includes knowing ethical principles and standards, especially those appropriate to each person's profession and condition. Such knowledge requires the study of ethics, listening to moral voices in society regarding specific issues and personal reflection. Ethical criteria acquired from similar situations are also part of the *training of the conscience.*

■ *Practical wisdom* (*prudence*, in a moral sense), which, as noted (see pp. 40–42), helps one to judge with moral rectitude, is acquired over time. It reinforces practical reason in making moral judgments, and so in solving moral dilemmas. Practical wisdom applies universal ethical principles (see pp. 28–32) to the situation in hand. It also entails adopting a *sincere attitude* in seeking what is just and good, and avoiding the temptation to justify one's own interests. When the decision-maker has serious doubts, practical wisdom leads him or her to seek advice from suitable people, that is, those competent regarding the matter in question and of proven moral character. If doubt persists over what a sound moral judgment might be in a particular situation, a wise person will lean towards the safer judgment in moral terms. For instance, avoiding an additive in a food which may be a health risk, even if there is not conclusive evidence of its danger. Another example could be prudence in what constitutes reasonable protection of a worker against possible accidents.

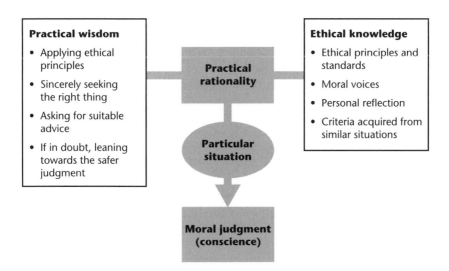

FIGURE 3.2   **Formulation of moral judgments in decision-making**

The more important the issue, the more diligently one must apply oneself to dispelling doubts and making a *good decision*. After having used all reasonable means, one must make a sincere and honest judgment. Then, conscience will either be *right* or *insurmountably wrong*, but it will be certain of the conclusion and so will have to be obeyed.

MAKING SOUND MORAL JUDGMENTS

There are ethical theories which take a different path for making moral judgments than the one presented here. In Chapter 2 we mentioned some theories based on principles and virtue-based theories (see pp. 26–27). Among the former there are two mainstream groups of theories: theories based on duties (Deontologism) and theories which stand for evaluating and balancing the consequences of every action (Consequentialism, among which Utilitarianism is prominent).

Ethical theories and moral reasoning

Deontological theories are centered on duties (*deon* in Greek means "duty") which are accepted *prima facie*, that is, as rationally self-evident. Kant, a genuine proponent of a well-known stream of Deontologism, saw moral duties as being derived from a categorical imperative, the justification of which is its capacity of becoming universal. It is questionable that, by the mere fact that a norm has become universal, it is a moral duty. It is also open to question that consequences and other circumstances of the action are not taken into account and, what is more, duties remain separate from the human good and virtues. *Codes of conduct* are a typical product of this approach. These often present duties which are quite consistent with common morality and could be useful in pointing out certain minimum standards. However, a pure deontological approach to decision-making falls short in the lack of consideration it gives to the role of the decision-maker's moral character and to the weighing up of consequences, and also in the disconnection it produces between duties and human flourishing.

Utilitarianism focuses on *goods* obtained as consequences of the action, measured in terms of utility or satisfaction of those who are affected by such consequences and applying an axiomatic principle that an action is ethical when it produces the greatest happiness (satisfaction) for the greatest number. This system presents several problems. The first is to identify utility and satisfaction with moral good. This is contrary to the common understanding of morality. Sometimes good behavior requires the sacrifice of utility and hedonistic satisfaction. Another difficulty with utilitarianism is that it reduces morality to an arithmetical calculation of utilities, which is not only quite difficult but also inconsistent with the notion of intentionality (see pp. 57–63).

A third objection is the lack of consideration in this theory for the rights of minorities: the greatest satisfaction for the greatest number can lead to violation of the human rights of the minority.

A third approach, known as *virtue ethics*, has become quite popular in the last two decades. It focuses on the moral character of the agent and its influence in making correct judgments, but some contemporaneous theories on virtue ethics show its serious limitations. Some of these understand virtues within a cultural context, and this entails relativism and a lack of connection with true human excellence. Others see virtues as traits of character which lead to better efficiency in business. In this case, they may confuse operative habits – such as being a hard worker, or even a workaholic, or being astute – with moral character, which only leads to good behavior. On the other hand, some criticize virtue ethics because it does not present specific duties and it is difficult to look for accountability from a virtue ethics perspective.

All of these theories have some aspect of truth and present relevant but incomplete aspects regarding ethics in decision-making, namely in the consideration of moral duties and consequences associated with an action and the role of virtues.

There is another theory which is more comprehensive than these, since it includes all of these elements – virtues, duties and consequences – in a consistent way with the principles, values and virtues enumerated in the previous chapter. In this theory, called the *Triple Font of Morality*, the intentionality of the decision-maker is central, and this covers both the intention of an end and the election of a means for this end, as well as the consequences and other circumstances. We will discuss it next.

The Triple Font of Morality Theory

Every decision entails deliberation and election of an end, and an action chosen as a means to achieve that end. Thus, the will of the decision-maker concerns both the end and the means. In addition, sound deliberation cannot ignore the predictable consequences of the action and other morally relevant situational circumstances. These three elements are fonts or sources to evaluate the morality of a decision or a human act (see Figure 3.3).

- *Intention*: morality of purpose or goal for which the decision is taken.
- *Action chosen*: morality of the action chosen as a means to the end.
- *Circumstances*: morality of relevant consequent circumstances (*predictable consequences* of the action) and antecedent circumstances (*situational factors*).

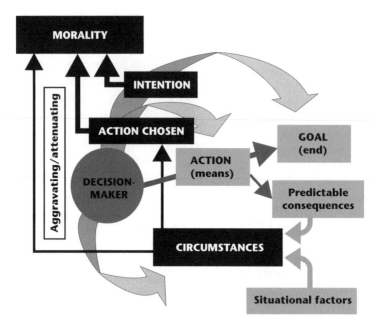

FIGURE 3.3 **Moral evaluation of a decision**

The Triple Font of Morality Theory holds that a decision is morally good if, and only if, all of these elements are good. Regarding the meaning of the action chosen it is worth making a clarification. Action chosen denotes a choice made with *rational knowledge of its morality*. This term excludes any purely empirical consideration of the means, which is often a source of considerable confusion. Thus, "murder" and "killing in legitimate defense" are ethically different, although both of them correspond to the same physical act (killing). In order words, the *action chosen* has moral significance, since it involves a moral evaluation. This is often expressed by language. The action chosen can be, for instance, an (honest) sale, or a fraud, or maybe a bribe, a misrepresentation, or whatever. The action chosen, in classic terminology, is termed *object chosen*, or simply *object*, because this is the "object chosen by the will" – and therefore intentional – as a means to an end.

The rationale for the Triple Font of Morality Theory is the following. The intention and the object chosen are two aspects of the single voluntary act of making a decision. It is an internal act of the decision-maker which will be materialized when it is put into effect; but, in essence, the action exists already in the decision-maker's mind from the moment he or she makes the decision.

The unity of intention and action chosen can be illustrated by the following example. Suppose that, with the *intention* of saving a company from bankruptcy, various possible alternatives or external acts are being considered. Each alternative may be analyzed from the ethical point of view; some may be morally acceptable, while others may not (a fraud, for example). In the end, one alternative is *chosen*. Externally, all that we see is the act itself, but in the decision-maker's mind the intention and the action chosen are a single act. The complete action would be defined as "committing fraud to save the company", which expresses the inseparable unity between end and means in this decision.

The *unity* of the intention (end) and the choice of an alternative (means) leads to the conclusion that a decision is morally correct if, and only if, both the intention and the chosen means are good. In other words, the good demands that all its elements be good; by contrast, for something to be bad, any defect is sufficient.

We thus arrive at the popular saying: "the end does not justify the means". Although, in fact, it would be more accurate to say that a *good end does not justify morally bad means*. This precision is necessary since the means have to be carefully analyzed in order to determine that they are truly "bad means". Sometimes, the context can lead one to conclude that a certain means which is not generally acceptable could be so in certain circumstances. This is why a serious aggression in legitimate defense with proportionate means facing an aggressor is morally justified when there are no other resources to avoid such an aggression (notice, however, how many requisites are required to justify a means). Some people may maintain that the end justifies the means. This is the case with Niccolò Machiavelli (see pp. 89–90), who justified both good and not so good means to maintain political power. But accepting this statement justifies power, in its different forms, over human rights and so justifies practically everything to obtain it. Subordinating ethics to any interest destroys the proper sense of ethics, which is precisely to evaluate the moral acceptability of interests. Accepting that the end justifies the means may have unpredictable consequences for organizations and for society. As the French writer, Georges Bernanos, said, "the first sign of corruption in a society that is still alive is that the end justifies the means".[8]

Thus, intention and the action chosen are two key fonts of morality. The third font of morality (circumstances) adds the morality of predictable consequences of the decision (consequent circumstances) and situational circumstances.

Certain consequences can change a generically good action into one that is bad (e.g., when disproportionate and negative consequences occur). In addition, some situational circumstances can change the action chosen substantially, adding special seriousness. Thus, murdering a father or mother is known as *parricide*. In a business context, *embezzlement* is distinguished from *swindle*. While the latter means to defraud of money or property, the former entails taking property (money) from a person who is in a position of trust, such as a manager or employee. In contrast, and more commonly encountered, are circumstances that do not change the action chosen (*object*) itself substantially, but aggravate or attenuate the seriousness of it (e.g., the amount of money stolen). Thus, the morality of a decision is basically determined by intention and the action chosen and complemented by the consideration of consequences and situational circumstances, which aggravate or attenuate its seriousness.

Determining the morality of a decision

Now the question is how to determine the morality from these fonts. As noted, according to the Triple Font of Morality Theory, a sound moral judgment must consider these three elements of morality: (1) intention, (2) action chosen and (3) circumstances, including predictable consequences and situational factors.

Intention

For an intention to be *good* it must be directed toward a good end. That means the intention must be oriented toward a goal that is consistent with the dignity and rights of persons and contributes to human flourishing, or at least not preventing it.

The intention may target one or more proximate ends of the action, or it may extend to other ends more remote from the most immediate ones. For example, a salesperson may make a sale in order to earn a commission, to satisfy the customer, to win the customer's confidence, to render a genuine service, to contribute to the upkeep of his or her own family and so on. One or other of these ends will be the *ultimate end* with respect to the others. The ultimate end sets the priority when different ends turn out to be incompatible (for example, in the short term, earning a commission on the sale may not be compatible with rendering a genuine service to the customer: one of these two ends, therefore, will be the ultimate end with respect of the other).

The moral quality of the intention may have different degrees of intensity: the intention will be better or worse depending on the ethical value of the purpose for which the action is done. The more valuable the end of the action desired by the will, the better the intention. Thus, to act to *earn money honestly* is a good intention, but the moral quality of the intention will be greater if the action is performed in a *spirit of service*, even to the extent that the person who acts gives others the same consideration as him or herself.

Action chosen (object)

The morality of the action chosen is determined by reference to the human good, and, more specifically, to the immediate moral duties or rules derived from ethical values and principles that we referred to in Chapter 2 (see pp. 28–40).

In this evaluation, we might find the action chosen is ethically unacceptable for one or more of the following reasons:

1. The action is *radically contrary* to human dignity or the common good. These types of actions are prohibited by negative moral norms and are qualified as *intrinsically wrong actions*, unacceptable with no exceptions. They include, for instance, slavery, fortunately abolished in most parts of the world, and whatever else that can be easily recognized as ignominious working conditions and mistreatment (see pp. 81–83), bearing false witness and perjury, and violation of certain fundamental rights that can never be relinquished, such as the right to life of an innocent, protection of health, the right to a fair trial, the right to seek the truth, the right not to be defamed by untruths (calumnies). In commerce, we can mention, among others, theft, fraud, lies, manipulation of people through persuasion with lies, bribe and extortion. It is worth noting that these concepts have in their corresponding definition, an element that delimits what is intrinsically wrong. Thus, for example, *theft* is usurping another's property without the *reasonable* will of the owner; a lie is an untruthful statement with *an intention* to deceive others who have the right to know the truth. There are situations in which it could be ethically acceptable to make a false statement with the intention of protecting a legitimate secret from an "unjust aggressor", but this would not be a lie in the moral sense, but an act of *legitimate self-defense*.
2. The action is not allowed by a fair law, and consequently is *illegal*. Generally these actions include the previous group, but there are many other regulations through which the legitimate authority specifies generic ethical principles or establishes requirements for a harmonious and just social life. Unless solid arguments and the agreement of recognized moral voices exist to the contrary, there is a presumption that any law is fair. A law would be not fair, however, if it was contrary to human dignity and rights or to any other superior ethical requirement.

3. The action is *wrong in some specific circumstances*. These actions could be acceptable in some circumstances but not in others, according to sound criteria or the good judgment of wise persons. This is the case for certain rights, and the corresponding duties of justice, which may yield to other rights, or to the common good in certain circumstances. For example, the rights of the owner of a piece of land may yield to the need to build a road (legitimate expropriation for the common good). However, so long as it is not solidly proven that a certain right has yielded to another, that right must be respected, and any infringement of that right will constitute an unacceptable action (not respecting a person's ownership rights gives rise to an *action chosen* such as theft, fraud, etc.).
4. The action is unjust because it *lacks equity or due proportion*. For example, disciplinary action taken against a worker is not bad in itself. It may even be very good if it has a salutary effect and is in proportion to the misdemeanor. But it may be unjust if the punishment is disproportionate to the misdemeanor and the supposed salutary effect.

Relevant consequences and situational factors

Beginning with situational factors, as noted (see p. 60), some of them can change the object chosen substantially, or, more commonly, they can aggravate or attenuate the seriousness of the action.

More complex can be the evaluation of the consequences, especially when the action chosen produces good effects but also bad effects (usually called *secondary* or *side effects*). Typical examples of secondary effects are pollution, lay-offs resulting from corporate restructuring, and risks of industrial accidents in dangerous jobs, to mention just a few. To refer to these as side effects is not to say that they are unimportant (they may be extremely important), merely that they are not directly intended. They are indirectly voluntary.

In the evaluation of actions with secondary effects, we must take into account that the decision-maker is responsible for predictable and avoidable consequences of a licit action from which it is expected that a greater good will be obtained. Under this premise, an action with both good and bad effects – *an action of "double effect"* – would be ethically permissible in the following conditions:

1. There are no other *permissible alternatives* that are *better* and *feasible*. It would not be prudent to inquire into the lawfulness of a course of action without first having deliberated sufficiently about other possible solutions.

2. *The action chosen is licit*, that is, it is generically good or indifferent. The reason for this condition is that it is never permissible to do wrong directly.
3. A bad consequence can only ever be tolerated as an *indirectly* willed effect, because it is an *inevitable effect* that accompanies or follows an action that in itself is good or indifferent. The good effect must be produced directly by the action, not by the bad effect; otherwise, the bad effect would, in fact, be the object of the action.
4. There is a proportionately grave cause of the bad consequences. However, if the latter are out of proportion to the need to perform the action, the action may be rendered ethically unacceptable.

These four conditions are necessary to accept that a decision is ethically correct with both good and bad effects concurring in an action. Condition 4 needs particular care. Let us consider a classic, highly illustrative example of the "double effect": the slaying of an unjust aggressor. Here, the action chosen is *legitimate self-defense*, which can be reasonably distinguished from *murder* and other forms of homicide. Legitimate self-defense is an action that cannot reasonably be said to be intrinsically bad. The principal effect (good effect) is the saving of one's own life, yet a further consequence is the death of the assailant (bad effect). The question of whether the slaying of an unjust aggressor is ethically acceptable can be answered as follows: it depends – in some circumstances, yes; in others, no. For example, if a madman started shooting indiscriminately at children coming out of a school, it would be reasonable to kill him if that were the only way to prevent a massacre. On the other hand, if it were possible to subdue the aggressor without killing him, then taking his life would not be reasonable and such an action would lose its legitimacy: it would be illegitimate self-defense. This simple example demonstrates how bad side effects are tolerable only if there is a proportionately grave reason for permitting them.

ETHICAL ANALYSIS OF THE MORALITY OF A DECISION WITH BAD SECONDARY EFFECTS

In a practical way, and bearing in mind all that has been said, seven stages can be suggested to analyze the morality of a decision. These guidelines can help in formulating moral judgments especially in decisions in which bad secondary or side effects are predictable. We present these stages as questions for the decision-maker (Figure 3.4):

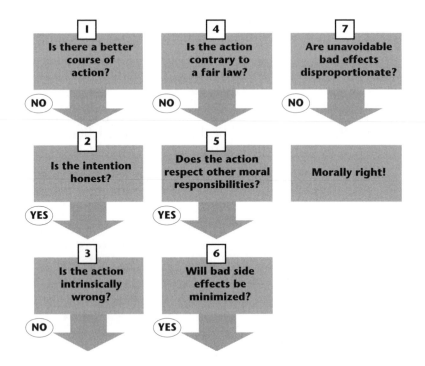

FIGURE 3.4   **Stages for complex moral judgments in decision-making**

Stage 1: Is there a better course of action?
This question is particularly important when it is predictable that some bad effects can occur in implementing the decision. Maybe another course of action could have less serious side effects. This question also makes sense in seeking a better and more feasible course of action. Very often, using creativity and professional competence, it is possible to come up with a better alternative that provides a way out of the stark choice between "do this" or "do nothing".

Stage 2: Is the intention honest?
As noted above, intention is one of the key elements for evaluating the morality of a decision. An upright or honest intention requires *willingness to do good* and *sincerity* in determining what the side effects really are, and not confusing them with the direct consequences of the action. For example, where profits have been made by fraudulent means, it would not be reasonable to say that deceiving the buyers is a side effect. Actually, this is an immediate consequence of the fraud.

The bad effects must be genuinely unavoidable. Honest intention demands that bad effects are not directly intended, but merely *tolerated* as an unavoidable *lesser evil*.

Stage 3: Is the action intrinsically wrong?
As noted above, there are actions which are intrinsically wrong, and this is the next question to ask. If the action involves fraud, deception, lying or a lack of respect for human dignity and rights, for example, it should be rejected.

Stage 4: Is the action contrary to a fair law?
If the action is not allowed by a fair law, it should also be rejected, as noted (see p. 62), since laws passed by a legitimate authority have an ethical content, specifying generic ethical duties or establishing requirements for a harmonious and just social law.

Stage 5: Does the action respect other moral responsibilities?
An action can be ethically unacceptable, not only because it is intrinsically wrong or illegal, but also because it does not respect other moral responsibilities, including *positive duties* (see p. 52) of doing good and avoiding bad effects as much as possible. In carrying out the evaluation of this point, a *stakeholder analysis* can be useful, that is, considering who will be affected, for good or bad, by the decision.

Stage 6: Will bad secondary effects be minimized?
Uprightness in intention requires the willingness to use all *reasonable means to minimize the secondary effects* using available technical resources and human skills to minimize them as far as possible in each situation. If the decision-maker does not take reasonable steps to prevent these, the side effects cannot be considered unintended.

Stage 7: Are unavoidable bad effects disproportionate?
The need to perform the action must be proportionate to the unavoidable bad effects that will flow from the action. The judgment as to such proportionality must be a prudential rather than a utilitarian judgment. It is not a matter of weighing up the pros and cons, based on physical or economic goods, as in the case of cost–benefit analysis, nor of weighing up advantages and disadvantages in any utilitarian fashion, but of prudentially weighing the moral goods (good and bad) that will result from the action.

In making the judgment about proportionality, the decision-maker should consider the *seriousness* of *the bad effect* versus the *cause of the necessity* to perform the action in the light of ethical standards. Another criterion is the *causal proximity* between the act and the side effects, which can be further consequences progressively distant from the action. The more distant the consequences are from the action, the less responsibility there will be for them.

The judgment on proportionality may be difficult to formulate at times. The challenge is to judge *impartially*, without letting one's *own interests* induce one to rationalize the situation to justify selfish postures. The Golden Rule (see pp. 28–29) in doing this is to *put oneself in the other person's position*, and consider that the *goods of the person* are common to the one who decides and to those who receive the effects of the decision. In doubtful cases, practical wisdom demands that one *seek advice* from honest and level-headed experts. By doing so, one will have an independent, qualified opinion, thus avoiding the disadvantages that arise when one has to make a judgment while also being an interested party.

SOLVING ETHICAL DILEMMAS

Ethical dilemmas emerge in decision-making when there is an apparent mental conflict between two duties, in such a way that to follow one would entail transgressing the other. In this type of situation, managers may feel unsure about what is the correct thing to do, because it can seem impossible to comply with both duties at once. Sometimes, one of the two duties is actually a *pseudo-duty* and in discovering it the dilemma is solved. In other cases the dilemmas can be solved with a solution that harmonizes both duties. Other dilemmas are more complex and require sound reasoning about which duty might have priority.

Ethical duty versus obeying orders

There may sometimes appear to be a conflict between a negative ethical duty (a moral prohibition) and the duty to obey orders of one's superiors. This could be the case, for example, of a manager or an employee who is asked to participate in some "dirty business" or to falsify specifications of a product. Another situation, which entails a similar dilemma, could be with a course of action which is not ethical but it seems in the best economic interest of the company. The case, for example, of a manager who thinks of paying a bribe to obtain a contract. In a certain sense, in this second case, the manager obeys an implicit order to favor the bottom line or to show "loyalty" to his or her company.

In these situations, the duty to obey orders is only a moral duty when such an order is morally legitimate, which is not the case of making money through corrupt means or, similarly, of falsifying a product specification. Neither can a bribe be justified by saying that it is for the best interests of the company for which the manager works, and not for personal gain, because one cannot do wrong to achieve a good (see pp. 59–60). Apart from the questionable matter of whether this will truly be in the best interests of the company, this is not a moral duty. No appeal to loyalty as justification is possible either since, in ethical terms, loyalty is not a virtue when it entails doing wrong (this is the case of *pseudo-loyalty* to the Mafia or a band of robbers).

In situations where an ethical duty conflicts with obeying orders, the main difficulty may be in having the strength to refuse to obey the command and to take appropriate measures to solve the dilemma. Among the measures possible might be presenting a *conscientious objection* or reporting the case to a higher level within the organization. In extreme cases, the situation might require telling the authorities or the public that the organization you are working for is doing something immoral or illegal (*whistle-blowing*).

In the hypothetical case of obeying orders that have some basis in unfair laws, legal duties yield to ethical duties, since laws are subordinate to ethics.

More complicated may be the dilemma of a mandated action that is not bad in itself, such as obeying instructions to produce a document that is then used by another person to get a contract using bribery. If the purpose is known this entails certain *moral cooperation* with an illicit action. Similarly, working for a company in which one or more products damage human flourishing (e.g., certain video games for children), where one is not directly involved in such products nor approves of them, but, in some way, collaborates in a more or less remote manner (managing accounting or the finances of the company, for instance). The best solution here would be to work for a company where such moral cooperation is not necessary, but sometimes this can be difficult. In this latter situation there is what some ethicists term a *material cooperation* (unapproved) in wrongdoing. This could be acceptable if, when weighing up the seriousness of the bad effects in which one cooperates, they are inferior to the necessity to remain in the company and one's own actions are far removed from the bad effects the company causes. In more generic terms, material cooperation in wrongdoing can be acceptable in extreme cases, when a serious and proportionate need exists to cooperate and there is no other realistic alternative available.

Dilemmas with irregular payments

Bribery is one of the usual words to express irregular payments and corruption. Another is extortion. A *bribe* has been defined as "money or favors given or promised to influence the judgment or conduct of a person in a position of trust".[9] The person who receives the bribe has power or influence over a decision which can be favorable to the one who pays the bribe or to a third party. *Bribery*, understood as the act or practice of giving or taking a bribe, can involve managers, business officials, civil servants, politicians, judges and people in other positions on both sides of the exchange, giving or taking. The matter might entail obtaining a contract or a license, selling a product, getting a favorable legal decision or accelerating administrative procedures.

Extortion is the act or practice of obtaining money or other property by force, intimidation, or undue or illegal power. In the business context extortion is sometimes expressed by saying "asking for a bribe". However, the term extortion is more correct to indicate someone (head of purchasing, a civil servant, etc.) who abuses his or her power to require money for doing his or her work or to make a decision favorable to those who are extorted. One blatant form of extortion is a terrorist group or a criminal band who demand money under the threat of causing damage to company facilities, products and even people (e.g., kidnap).

The question of paying or not paying a bribe is easily solved by rejecting such practices, since bribery is an act of injustice by those who take the money to which they have no right. To extort is also completely unacceptable ethically, and a crime. It is also unacceptable to give in to an extortionist to obtain a favor unfairly.

The main dilemma arises when a person or a business firm is extorted for something to which they are entitled, such as obtaining a contract in a fair competition or a license in due time. What can one do in these situations? Could it be ethically acceptable to give in to extortion when one has a right to something but apparently the only way to obtain it is by giving in to extortion? What can one do, for instance, when an organized group threatens to kidnap your children if you do not pay them and the police in the country are none too effective? Obviously, as in other dilemmas, first of all it is necessary to find alternatives to get out of the dilemma, but what if these alternatives do not exist or are not effective?

When someone suffers extortion, he or she is not taking an active role, but, on the contrary, is the victim of an unfair action. However, in giving in to extortion there is a certain cooperation in wrongdoing, although it is not a *formal cooperation* (with approval) but only *material cooperation* (without approval). As noted (see p. 67), material cooperation in wrongdoing can be acceptable in extreme cases and under certain strict conditions, but without forgetting that cooperation spreads corruption and there is a positive duty to fight against it.

Conflict between two ethical duties

When conflict arises between two ethical duties, one negative and the other positive, the negative duty – what is not allowed – is always binding and must be obeyed first. Put in generic terms: first, do not damage; second, try to serve. Negative duties are minimum requirements that come first.

A different problem arises when positive duties come into conflict with one another. A simple example would be the case of an executive who faces the dilemma of either staying at home to look after a sick child, or attending to some business that is vital in order to win an important contract. In many situations such as this, the two duties could be reconciled by finding alternatives or explaining the situation to the relevant person and negotiating a reasonable solution (the executive's spouse or the grandparents could no doubt look after the child as well as he or she could, or the business could perhaps be postponed without any very serious consequences). If that is not possible, one has to prudently weigh up the objective importance of the respective duties and their foreseeable consequences, and omit the least important of them. That decision will give rise to side effects that are tolerated as inevitable in performing an action that has sufficient necessary cause. Thus, in solving dilemmas like this, practical wisdom is crucial.

Another dilemma is related to situations in which tackling a problem entails a greater ill. Imagine a factory where one of the employees is not performing as he or she should, but there is general unrest and considerable tension due to other problems. Here, there is also a conflict between two positive duties: the duty to correct the employee, and the duty to cultivate peaceful industrial relations in the company. In view of the specific situation, it may be prudent to postpone the correction so as not to inflame the atmosphere. The solution to this dilemma is known as *tolerance of a lesser evil*. Although doing wrong is neither allowed nor recommended, even when others do it, in some circumstances it is morally permissible to tolerate wrong in the interest of a higher good or to avoid more serious disorders. A temporary tolerance of an incorrect situation to avoid higher evils can be justified, and may even be morally obligatory, but it should be kept under review since circumstances can change.

Notice that solving dilemmas through the lesser evil approach is not a matter of choosing the lesser of two evils, since doing wrong can never be morally obligatory. One must do *what is right and tolerate* the lesser evil as an inevitable side effect.

EXECUTIVE SUMMARY

The decision-making process has a set of well-known stages, including formulation of the problem, outlining a goal and outcome, generation of alternative courses of action, analysis and evaluation of these alternatives, election of one alternative, implementation of this and evaluation of the outcome.

Social sciences, and particularly sociology and psychology, have paid great attention to managerial behavior, including how managers make decisions. Here we take a different approach by asking how to make good decisions by considering their ethical dimension, though not forgetting that a decision has other dimensions. We consider four: the *instrumental dimension* related to business results; the *relational dimension*, which regards the future relations with people affected by the action; the *internal dimension* or learning produced in the decision-maker; and the *ethical dimension*, which refers to the ethical evaluation of the decision. These dimensions are different but interdependent, in the sense that a dimension can affect others in future decisions.

A holistic approach to decision-making entails considering different evaluative criteria for each dimension: cost–benefit analysis (instrumental), pros and cons for future relations (relational), development and degradation of internal capabilities and motivations (internal), and right and wrong; better and worse (ethical). A minimum in each dimension is required and this leads us to reject some alternatives for some reason: as not economically viable, unacceptable for the social environment, contrary to decision-maker growth, non-ethical. Considering the remaining alternatives, both short- and long-term consequences should be considered. Ethics take primacy over economic results because ethics focuses on human good, which entails an absolute priority over interests such as profitability, which are only an instrumental good; good for something, but not absolutely good. Positive duties depend on the possibilities in each situation. What may be good in the short-term can become bad in the long-term. Thus, choosing the best alternative requires practical wisdom and the weighing up of short-term and long-term effects in all dimensions.

Moral judgment (judgment of conscience) is an evaluation of a particular situation by practical reason using ethical knowledge and helped by practical wisdom.

The Triple Font of Morality Theory, proposed here, considers duties, consequences and virtues, in contrast with other theories that only focus on one of these elements. According to this theory, the moral evaluation of a decision includes three elements: *intention* (morality of the end or goal for which the decision is taken); *action chosen* (morality of the means for this end); and the morality of *relevant consequences and situational factors.* The *unity* of the end and the means leads to the conclusion that a decision is morally correct if, and only if, both the intention and the chosen means are good, or in popular terms, "the end does not justify the means".

In a practical way, a systematic analysis of the morality of a decision requires asking (1) if this is the best course of action or if it might be necessary to explore others, (2) if the intention is honest, (3) if the action is intrinsically wrong (unacceptable in any circumstance), (4) if the action is contrary to a fair law, (5) if the action respects other moral responsibilities, (6) if the negative side effects will be minimized, and (7) if unavoidable negative effects are proportionate to the necessity of performing the action.

The chapter concludes by discussing how to solve ethical dilemmas, including ethical duties versus obeying orders, dilemmas in irregular payments and conflict between ethical duties.

CHAPTER 4

CENTRALITY OF THE PERSON IN MANAGEMENT

Management is about human beings. Its task is to make people capable of joint performance, to make their strengths effective and their weaknesses irrelevant. This is what organization is all about, and it is the reason that management is the critical, determining factor.[1]

PETER F. DRUCKER (1909–2005)

Peter F. Drucker is recognized as the father of modern management and as one of the most prolific and influential authors in his field. Of Austrian origin, he obtained his doctorate in International Law in Germany, and in his formative years worked in the banking sector as a journalist. Emigrating to the USA in 1937, he practiced as a teacher and business consultant, but it was his writing on politics and society in the early 1940s that opened the door of General Motors to him, and gave him the opportunity to study their administration control systems at first hand. This early work translated into his famous book *The Concept of the Corporation* (1946), which contained the seed of many concepts he would go on to develop in later articles and books. His attention was drawn to the frequent capacity of the workers to contribute more with their minds than with their hands, knowing more at times than even their superiors. This phenomenon, in stark contrast to the dominant view of the time that workers simply had to follow orders, led Drucker to his vision of management where the person is of greater importance.

Management from its very beginnings focused on people to improve efficiency, trying to achieve goals using a minimum of resources. Some pioneers in the field also included elemental aspects of justice in their management principles. Thus, Frederick W. Taylor assumed that the employer should pay what had been agreed with the employee, and Henri Fayol's Administrative Principles include fair payment for services, justice in punishment for indiscipline, and equity – not necessarily equality – in dealing with workers. Over time methods to improve efficiency arrived, many of which were due to a better knowledge of human behavior. Justice was extended with the recognition of some labor rights and through new regulations.

In 1938, Chester I. Barnard, an influential management thinker, posited the importance of a deep understanding of the human being by saying: "I have found it impossible to go far in the study of organizations or of behavior of people in relation to them without being confronted with a few questions which can be simply stated. For example: 'What is an individual?' 'What is a person?' 'To what extent do people have power of choice or free will?'" Adding: "The temptation is to avoid such difficult questions, leaving them to philosophers and scientists who still debate them after centuries. It quickly appears, however, that even if we avoid answering such questions definitely, we cannot avoid them."[2]

This idea has been repeated from time to time by some management thinkers. "Nothing is more fundamental in setting our research agenda and informing our research methods" – wrote the Nobel Laureate Herbert Simon – "than our view of the nature of human beings whose behaviours we are studying ... It makes a difference to research, but it also makes a difference for the proper design of ... institutions".[3]

With the passing of years, Barnard's question of what the human individual is has translated into a better understanding of human behavior in organizations. Rather than a rational inquiry into human nature, experimental psychologists employed empirical methodology, modeling data taken from different samples of people and situations. Now there is a vast body of behavioral science, which tries to describe what human behavior is in particular situations and what the appropriate manner of treating people might be to contribute to better performance. This is useful, but limited. Science does not answer the deep questions of what the human being is, what being a person means, whether or not people have dignity and rights, or what kind of treatment a human being deserves.

In management studies, a rational understanding of the human being – focused on *what* a human being is – has received much less attention than behavioral science – focused on *how* humans act – and so a vacuum is created; a vacuum that can contribute to the substituting of models of individuals for the real person. As Barnard mentioned, the temptation is to avoid the difficult question about what a human being is, but if you do not face this question you will acritically assume a certain idea of the human being. This is the case of most current economic theories that consider a model of man, termed *homo oeconomicus*, focused on interests and preferences, which the individual tries to maximize through rationality, with the principal aim of evaluating and balancing costs and benefits. No other aspects of human rationality are considered.

This model has been severely criticized not only by philosophers, psychologists and sociologists, but also by economists, including the Nobel Laureates Amartya Sen and Joseph Stiglitz. Sen points out the limitation of the narrow rationality of the *homo oeconomicus* and the irrelevance in the model of human motivations as central as generosity or spirit of service.[4] On his part, Stiglitz holds that the idea of rational self-interest is not sufficient to explain economic behavior.[5] He also feels that "individuals and firms, in the pursuit of self-interest, are not necessarily, or in general, led as if by an invisible hand, to economic efficiency".[6] Sumantra Ghoshal, with many others, also stresses the risks of managing exclusively by means of the mainstream economic theories with their underlying model of people as rational self-interest maximizers.[7]

Research on human behavior is relevant for management, but when managers do not go beyond this, they may see employees as mere resources for profits and consumers as a simple source of income, not as individuals with a conscience, freedom and numerous possibilities for self-realization.

A rational understanding of the human being – even in elemental terms like those we will present here – can help to fill such a vacuum. It also fosters dealing with people in a proper way, avoiding seeing them as mere resources or simple means for profit. *Humanistic management* is about recognizing what people are, treating them accordingly and fostering their development.

AN UNDERSTANDING OF THE "PERSON"

Roman law used the term *person* to refer to a human individual, and *personal* with the meaning of being borne or possessed by a human individual. In the Middle Ages, the concept of person acquired the meaning of a subject who possessed reason, and it also expressed excellence.

In common language, *person* refers to a human being as distinct from an animal or a thing.[8] That is what language expresses by distinguishing "someone" from "something".[9] The meaning we will take here is just this, but adding the idea that *person* encompasses dignity and worthiness, which emphasizes that human beings are endowed with an absolute value which deserves full respect. Things have a price, people have dignity.

But what is a human being? Everybody has an intuitive notion of what a human being is, but this is actually a tough philosophical question to answer in any depth. We will not enter here into a sophisticated debate on human nature, but something succinct should be said for practical purposes.

Aristotle proposed as a constituent principle a key deep feature that only humans have in common, and which can explain other distinctive characteristics we find across the range of humans. This is the "rational principle" which makes them human.[10] From this, we have the classical definition of the human being as a *rational animal*. More precisely, we can say that the human is an *animal who possesses reason* (logos), a conceptual and discursive intelligence. This seems reasonable, inasmuch as other important human features, such as conscience, moral discernment, freedom and sociability may be understood as a consequence of rationality. Other thinkers, however, emphasize the role of the will and emotions to define the human being, holding that the human person is fundamentally a *passionate being*, stressing how important the emotions are in human life. This is the case of Augustine of Hippo, who, in the 5th century, held that the driver of personal life is *love*, understood in a wide sense, although reason also has its role in reflecting on personal self-interest and trying to discover what could be the most convenient. Related to this, some modern philosophers stress *freedom* and human autonomy in moral behavior even more than rationality. This also seems reasonable since freedom is a feature of the two superior capacities of the person traditionally mentioned by many philosophers: intellect and will. We can synthesize these positions in the definition of the human being as a *living being who possesses emotions, reason and freedom*.

Characteristics of the human being

Rationality and freedom

Humans have, however, much in common with animals in their corporality, and in their instincts, or "genetic endowments", expressed as inherent inclinations toward particular behaviors, but human behavior is more dependent on cognitive capacities. Even the human body has some peculiar characteristics which differ from the body of the animal. This includes walking upright and possessing a face which can express emotions, smile, and be used for expression through winking, grimacing and so on. The human face can convey human language in a way not possible with a snout, for instance. The human hand is also quite particular, adapted to gesticulate and able to perform complex mechanical techniques – and not just simple instinctive operations for sustenance and shelter – and to work following reasoned purposes.

Both rationality and free will underlie such human characteristics, but rationality and free will entail much more than this.

Rationality, the condition of being rational, entails having intellectual understanding of the external world and even of oneself, beyond empirical data. This means a capacity for abstraction and to deliver judgments. Due to their *rationality*, humans can know or consider concepts, such as beauty, peace and wisdom. Moreover, humans are capable of reasoning not only about external things, but also about themselves, and reflecting on oneself and on the deep meaning of one's own existence. Through self-knowledge and self-reflection, each person realizes that they have an inner privacy, a "self-possessed 'I'". This *self-possession* confers a rich inner life, or *intimacy*, upon the person. Human rationality also has the capacity to drive the action seeking efficiency (instrumental reason) and discern good and bad (practical reason).

Humans very often have the intuition of *transcendence*, something existing apart from, and not subject to, the limitations of the material universe; or a preeminent or supreme Divine Being to whom humans often relate and worship. Different forms of spirituality and religion express such a sense of transcendence.

Freedom is a crucial basic human feature, as is rationality. As noted, freedom leads both the human intellect and will. I think about something because it is my will to do so, and I act because I choose to do so. Making free choices is indeed an expression of *freedom*, but human freedom, in a deeper sense, denotes possessing the *self-determination* to think and act.

Related to freedom and rationality is *autonomy*. Etymologically, autonomy means one "who gives oneself their own law"; this refers to the law dictated by one's own conscience, and not as an unthinking response to an external stimulus. Humans have the capacity to discover ethical values and the moral law and apply them to specific situations. Some thinkers go further and understand autonomy as being creative of ethical values and even the moral law. Actually, as noted (see p. 29), ethical values and moral law should be discovered rather than invented or created. In this sense, human autonomy consists of deciding what one's own behavior will be, but not in deciding what the human good is. Autonomy connects rationality and free will, and shows the capacity of the rational individual to make deliberate and un-coerced decisions. Due to this autonomy humans are *responsible* and *accountable* for their actions.

Uniqueness but with shared nature and culturally influenced

The notion of *person* rather than "individual" expresses the uniqueness of every human being, since no human being is a mere undifferentiated individual or exemplar of an animal species. He or she is someone unique, and cannot be replaced by any other human being, except perhaps in the execution of certain mechanical tasks. Every person has his or her own intimacy, personhood, and character developed over time. Everyone also has a biography, a personal history, held in their inner self.

However, all persons have in common the human nature. What metaphysics considers "being human" – with the common features presented in this outline – is also accepted, from a different perspective, by biology, which has discovered individual differences within a common species (the *Homo sapiens* species).

Humans are endowed with a *genetic inheritance*, a set of features transmitted through genes that have been passed from parents to their children; each with a specific genetic code. This physical nature conditions health, physical development and personality. It even has an influence on behavior (a strong tendency to be aggressive, for instance; or the contrary). However, humans are not automatons, absolutely determined by their respective genetic code. This does have an influence, but the human individual remains free and autonomous in his or her acts. A human being not only has a genetic code but a biography built up with free acts.

Culture is another influential element in human behavior. We learn many things by imitation, particularly in our childhood, and we are immersed in one or more cultures or cultural environments where communication and interaction take place, and consequently influence our behavior. A cultural context includes a set of intangible elements, such as beliefs, ideas and values shared by a number of people, and tangible elements, including symbols, objects or technology used by these people. Like genetic inheritance, culture may condition individual behavior, but personal freedom plays its role, too. Thus, the ideological position of *determinism*, which says that human behavior has its origin exclusively in genetic inheritance or culture, would mean denying human freedom. On the contrary, we feel ourselves to be the owners of our decisions and actions. Society recognizes this reality by rewarding persons for merits and punishing in the case of wrongdoing.

Emotions, motivations and habits

Humans experience feelings and *emotions*, which, along with bodily needs, stimulate desires and trigger motivations to act. Motivations can appear spontaneously and we do not always follow them. Although, sometimes, human behavior is not especially reflective and we make judgments prompted by sentiments. However, we do have autonomy to decide whether or not to act, or to do one thing or another, by means of a conscious process.

In other words, alongside *spontaneous motivations*, a *rational motivation* appears regarding the convenience or not of following a spontaneous motivation. Rational deliberation combines with self-determination and permits one to decide whether or not to respond to a stimulus, or to choose among several alternative courses of action.

Human behavior depends on motivations, but acquired routines, skills and stable dispositions of character can also have an influence. Certain routines can be acquired unconsciously, like gestures or movements, or acquired without engaging in self-analysis when undertaking routine tasks. Other routines and particularly skills are acquired more consciously, the agent being aware of the learning associated with the actions. This is the case of many *operative habits* useful for life, such as skills for work or art, or for practicing sports. Intellectual and *moral habits* are also acquired by repeating actions with free choice and deliberation.

Moral habits or stable dispositions of character – virtues and vices – are acquired being aware of the goodness of the action, and are very relevant for ethical behavior, as noted before (see pp. 11–12). Moral virtues help the human will to foster desires which contribute to human flourishing or, on the contrary, to moderate desires which can impede such flourishing. We will return to this point below.

Relationability and sociability

The human being is *relational*, with the capacity to establish relationships with others and enrich their character and personhood through such relations. *Relationability* can be expressed in different feelings and a variety of forms of support for others, and can also serve in achieving one's own interests. Empathy, sympathy and affection for others are some of these feelings.

Empathy is feeling with someone, feeling a co-experience of the situation or emotional state of another. *Sympathy* entails feeling sorry or pity for others and supporting them with compassion and sensibility. Sympathy can become *affection* or fondness, a tender feeling toward another.

In their relationability, humans are also *dialogical beings*. They can share what they think or feel with others and establish intentional and friendly links with them. This can bring about strong bonds of unity. Dialogue literally means "a conversation between two persons", in which they can interchange thoughts, feelings and even other deep aspects of their inner self. In the dialogical process – from *dia*, across, and *logos*, word, speech, discourse – a *human language* provides a rich way to communicate and share with other humans and thus fosters the forming of mutual links.

Humans are social beings; they possess *sociability*, a feature related to the tendency to live together and the rational understanding of what this entails. Humans live in *society*, not in isolation, and often show a willingness to live together in an established order, with harmony, justice and peace. This is what constitutes what we call *civilization*.

The etymology of society provides an idea of its meaning. Society comes from the Latin *societas*, which means a "friendly association with others". It is related to another Latin word, *socius*, meaning "companion, associate, comrade or business partner". There are societies of which one is a natural member, such as the family into which one is born, or the political community (tribe, clan, city, nation, etc.) to which one belongs. Many other societies, however, are voluntary associations of people.

Human flourishing

Human beings undergo physical development, but, at the same time, they are open to moral self-development by acquiring what reinforces the noblest human capacities: intellect and will. These capacities are respectively related to the searching for truth and loving what one understands is truly good, even when this means self-sacrifice. Moral virtues reinforce these capacities and bring about *human flourishing*. Thus, human flourishing is obtained through virtues, which strengthen the capacity for knowledge in its deepest sense (wisdom) and for neighborly love. The latter, the measure of which is giving oneself generously to others to help them in their needs and development, is crucial to understanding what human flourishing is.

The human characteristics broadly described here, including self-possession, self-determination and intimacy, help to make human dignity evident.

A better understanding of human nature and the uniqueness and dignity of every human being certainly has practical consequences for sound management. We will reflect in the next sections on four of these. The first regards possessing a human quality in dealing with people; the second is about seeing the business firm as a community of persons with a specific mission; the third refers to some ethical requirements in managing people's work within the business firm, and the fourth focuses on building up a person-centered corporate culture.

MANAGING PEOPLE WITH A HUMAN QUALITY

Human quality refers to appropriateness to the human condition. In human relationships, showing a human quality in our dealings becomes an ethical cornerstone within organizations and also in commercial activity. The scope can be extended to the consideration of relationships with *stakeholders*, which include persons and groups of people who are in interdependence with the business firm and are affected by or can affect managerial decisions.

In management, five levels of human quality in dealing with people can be distinguished: (1) mistreatment, (2) indifference toward people, (3) respectful treatment, (4) concern for people's interests and (5) favoring mutual esteem and cooperation (see Figure 4.1).

The five levels of human quality

(1) Mistreatment: blatant injustice
Mistreatment of people is the lowest level of human quality in dealing with people. Within this level there are different degrees of seriousness but all of them are completely unacceptable from an ethical, and generally also legal, perspective.

Mistreatment refers to treating people in a harmful, injurious or offensive way. It can be done through words and deeds, always entails aggression and, within organizations, it is often due to an abuse of a certain position. The former includes speaking insultingly, harshly or using unkind or even insolent words. Words can also express belittling, hatred or a desire to humiliate. Regarding deeds, mistreatment involves all kinds of practice or customs which are generally considered inhuman – inappropriate to the human condition – from physical or psychological aggression to manipulation.

Exploitation in the workplace is a blatant form of mistreatment, and it can take the form of forced labor, child labor and indentured labor. A particular form of exploitation is what is colloquially known as "sweatshops". These are workshops or manufacturing facilities in which working conditions are extremely deficient, with long working hours, very low wages, dubious health and safety conditions, and excessive restrictions on labor rights. Workers usually have a strong necessity for a job to earn a living and there may be no other way than to accept such conditions. On the side of the consumer, one can also find examples of mistreatment especially in cases of weak consumer legislation or poor reinforcement of such legislation.[11]

Lack of respect for religious freedom or being coerced to act against one's own conscience are also significant mistreatments, as are psychological harassment and sexual harassment. These are forms of aggression which, unfortunately, are not infrequent in many organizations. One form of psychological harassment is *bullying* (or *mobbing*) which entails a mistreatment by coercing others by fear or threat. It is a consequence of *abuse of power* or authority through repeated acts over time by a more powerful individual or a group upon those who are less powerful. *Manipulation* of people includes any underhand influence on people through lies, deception or creating false expectations to generally gain benefit or power.

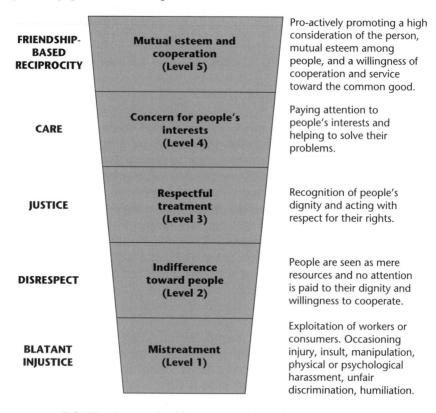

FRIENDSHIP-BASED RECIPROCITY	**Mutual esteem and cooperation (Level 5)**	Pro-actively promoting a high consideration of the person, mutual esteem among people, and a willingness of cooperation and service toward the common good.
CARE	**Concern for people's interests (Level 4)**	Paying attention to people's interests and helping to solve their problems.
JUSTICE	**Respectful treatment (Level 3)**	Recognition of people's dignity and acting with respect for their rights.
DISRESPECT	**Indifference toward people (Level 2)**	People are seen as mere resources and no attention is paid to their dignity and willingness to cooperate.
BLATANT INJUSTICE	**Mistreatment (Level 1)**	Exploitation of workers or consumers. Occasioning injury, insult, manipulation, physical or psychological harassment, unfair discrimination, humiliation.

FIGURE 4.1　**Levels of human quality within organizations**

Discrimination can be another significant aspect of mistreatment. Discrimination could be ethnic, racial, sexual, religious, political or social and also for reasons of age, gender and family situation. Although discrimination, meaning selection, has a negative connotation, it is not always unacceptable. A certain discrimination or selection is applied, for instance, in recruitment and promotion processes to fit the right person to the right job. What is not so acceptable is discriminating for reasons contrary to the equal dignity and innate rights of all persons.

All of these behaviors violate basic human rights and are, therefore, blatant injustices, contrary to the respect due to human dignity and to the Golden Rule (see pp. 28–31).

(2)   Indifference toward people: disrespect
On this second level of treatment there is no external mistreatment, but people do not receive any encouragement, emotional support, consideration or recognition. Legal requirements are generally met, but nothing is done beyond this; people are seen as mere resources with no attention paid to their dignity and their possible willingness to cooperate. People are used for economic ends, maybe employing some psychological technique to obtain more profitability from them, but without any consideration beyond this utilitarian goal. Indifference toward people can be a mindset which influences managers and other people within organizations in dealing with people.

Although there might be a tenuous distinction between abuse or mistreatment of people and indifference, some distinguishing features can be pointed out. A mindset of indifference can be shown by giving rough orders instead of asking respectfully; not listening to co-workers or not considering their feelings, experience and possible goodwill to cooperate; speaking without respect about other people's work or failing to give fair recognition when it may be due. Other examples could be responses that are given without any courtesy, or reasonable questions that receive "non-answers". There is no interest in people and no sensitivity toward whatever could concern people, including their problems and needs. People's spirituality or religious beliefs also meet with complete indifference in the workplace.

Those who act with indifference toward people may avoid calling them by name, thus devaluing their self-esteem; they may act without self-control or in angry outbursts, and this can generate negative feelings in collaborators. They may also make baseless internal judgments and criticisms of their target, even blaming people without solid evidence. In addition, their behavior can often be characterized by a lack of tolerance and in making jokes or speaking in a way that people may find offensive, and not sincerely apologizing for doing this.

Because of his or her human dignity, a person should never be treated as a thing or a mere resource for gains (see pp. 30–31). Neither should an interpersonal relationship be seen as a mechanism to achieve certain interests, without considering the other party as another "I".

A legal-based coexistence is too cold to express what is due to a human being. Indifference, understood as an absolute lack of affection, is not consistent with the Golden Rule (see pp. 28–29), and it shows disrespect for human dignity. Behaviors included on this level can be qualified, therefore, as disrespectful.

(3) Respectful treatment: justice

On this level, behaviors such as those described on levels 1 and 2 do not exist. On the contrary, on this level there is a recognition of people in their innate dignity and there is respect for their rights; not only legal rights, but also, and above all, their innate moral rights as human beings (human rights).

The third level is, therefore, characterized by justice (see pp. 33–36): give to each what is due, including respect and the promotion of human rights. Justice requires good use of power in dealing with people and in the corporate world. Most of the above-mentioned mistreatments have their origin in abuse[12] of power toward weak people or people in need, or abuse of a dominant situation.

Many companies are committed to respecting human rights even when operating in countries where such rights are not always guaranteed. They are explicit about their commitment to respecting people and their human rights. This can appear in their corporate statements (mission, values or codes of conduct) and/or they might adopt and publicize international standards such as the *UN Global Compact,* which includes ten principles in the areas of human rights, labor, the environment and anti-corruption (see Table 4.1).[13]

Justice includes keeping one's word, honoring contracts and agreements, including minor ones, and fairness in remuneration and performance appraisal, and indeed, in every other managerial system. Honesty in communication, avoiding the possibility of creating false expectations and respect for the truth are among many other expressions of justice.

Justice in managerial behavior also means equity, avoiding an unaccountable and arbitrary use of authority. Just behavior requires, for instance, that confidential information is not circulated beyond those authorized; that trade secrets are not revealed or internal information misused in order to give an advantage in investment (insider trading). Justice also means acting in such a way that confidence may be promoted, preventing any breach of confidence inherent in a position or relationship.

(4) Concern for people's interests: care

This level expresses acting toward people not only with recognition and respect, but also showing concern for their interests and compassion for their problems. This requires care as a response to another person, paying attention to his or her needs, problems and legitimate interests (see pp. 38–39).

Area	Principles
Human rights	*Principle 1:* Businesses should support and respect the protection of internationally proclaimed human rights; and *Principle 2:* make sure that they are not complicit in human rights abuses.
Labor standards	*Principle 3:* Businesses should uphold the freedom of association and the effective recognition of the right to collective bargaining; *Principle 4:* the elimination of all forms of forced and compulsory labor; *Principle 5:* the effective abolition of child labor; and *Principle 6:* the elimination of discrimination in respect of employment and occupation.
Environment	*Principle 7:* Businesses should support a precautionary approach to environmental challenges; *Principle 8:* undertake initiatives to promote greater environmental responsibility; and *Principle 9:* encourage the development and diffusion of environmentally friendly technologies.
Anti-corruption	*Principle 10:* Businesses should work against corruption in all its forms, including extortion and bribery.

TABLE 4.1 **Principles of the UN Global Compact**

On this level there is recognition of the worth of each person and their inner feelings, self-awareness and capacity for self-determination. Empathy and sympathy can contribute to this purpose. *Emotional intelligence* or the ability to identify, assess and control one's emotions, those of others and of groups can also be useful.

Like in level 3, on this level people are not seen as simple resources for personal or corporate interests, but as intrinsically worthy beings. Level 4 would make no sense without respect for human dignity and rights. Thus, this level includes what is required in level 3 but goes beyond justice, applying good feelings and intelligent love.

Authentic care excludes *hypocritical behaviors* such as using the appearance of interest and concern as a tactic for some kind of gain, or to obtain collaboration. In contrast with level 2, here there is a real concern for people, their vulnerability, problems, interests and needs.

Although the details of dealing with people with care depend on circumstances, on this level of human quality managers pay attention to people, considering their wellbeing and also the particular situations and needs of each one.

In the last decade an increasing interest has emerged in ethics focused on forms of concern for others and for their interests, and to extents that go beyond strict duties of justice. This was the case of the 2010 *Academy of Management* Meeting in Montréal, Canada, attended by thousands of people, the theme of which was "dare to care". The rationale of this conference was remembering that the role of management "is one of integration in all senses of the word – integrating the interests of all parties and integrating passion for one's work with compassion for others impacted by one's work".[14]

Managing with care for people refers especially to those closer to one's activity and people who are affected by managerial decisions. It focuses on enabling others to create, produce and deliver goods and services that enhance the wellbeing of, and generate value for, all the stakeholders involved (notably customers, employees, investors and the public). But care, driven with intelligent love, does not forget business sustainability. This is why managers should expand their focus toward an understanding of how solving organizational problems might ensure a sustainable future.[15]

(5) Mutual esteem and cooperation: friendship-based reciprocity
On this level of human quality concern is not limited to justice and care, but to pro-actively promoting a high consideration of the person and concern for personal development, mutual esteem among people, and a willingness for cooperation and service toward the common good.

This level of human quality may not be too common in many organizations. However, mutual esteem, reciprocal cooperation among people and a real and effective sense of service may be intense in some working teams or groups of people and less intense for the whole organization, especially when it is large. Transformational leadership, when it fosters these values, can be included in this level, with leaders who prioritize the seeking and promotion of the common good of the organization over their personal interests, and who try to transform their followers by nurturing their disposition to cooperation and service.

This level of human quality, as noted, includes respect for human dignity and rights and also compassion or concern for people's problems and interests, but it goes beyond this. It requires, first of all, fostering a vision of the wholeness and richness of the person and his or her possibilities of flourishing.

Reciprocity is key on this level, but a type of reciprocity which is limited neither to a commutative contract nor to a social contract, whereby something is given so that something may be received in return. Instead of an exchange of equivalents (or any *quid pro quo*), reciprocity on this level entails certain gratuitousness based on a sense of mutual esteem among those who cooperate with common goals, a certain sense of friendship. Thus this reciprocity is a *friendship-based reciprocity*. Rooted in the Aristotelian tradition, it stresses that humans are not only individuals with interests and preferences, but also social and cooperative beings, and able to build up communities based on goodwill and a sense of generosity, not only in contracts, either formal, psychological, or in what in political thought is understood by a "social contract".

This is a friendship-based reciprocity closely related to intelligent love (see pp. 38–40), and requires fostering mutual sympathy and esteem within the organization and with those with whom one interacts; as well as trying to develop the best of each member in a sense of service and cooperation. Seeing the business enterprise as a community of persons is fully consistent with corporate friendship and the corresponding reciprocity. We will consider this in the next section along with some attendant implications for management.

MANAGING THE BUSINESS ENTERPRISE AS A COMMUNITY OF PERSONS

Business firms (corporations or business enterprises) are usually identified as "organizations". This provides a view of an important aspect of what business enterprises are, but actually they are much more than this. Organization comes from the Latin *organum* "instrument, organ" and usually also has the meaning of "system" or "establishment".[16] In economic theory, the firm is often considered as an instrument supported by a set of contracts, while in sociology, the idea of a system of interests and the role of power are particularly stressed.

In a business firm there are obviously contracts and interests which unite people, and sometimes bring about conflicts, too; and power has, of course, its role. But there are other relevant elements which come together in building up this human reality of the business enterprise. Within a business firm, people work together in a coordinated and cooperative manner, although people can have different individual motives for working together, and they are united by several types of links.

Links which unite people (managers, employees, shareholders, suppliers, customers and so on) within and around the firm are usually very complex. There are, of course, contractual links and relationships based on mutual interests, but there can also be emotional links (shared sense of belonging, affection for one's work in the corporation) and moral links (commitment, moral loyalty, willingness to work for the common good of the firm, etc.). People who join a corporation find themselves, once hired, members of a social reality and over time a number of links can appear.

Thus, beyond describing the firm as a set of contracts or a system of interests, a more complete view can be proposed by considering that people are social beings; not only individuals with interests and power, but also with a capability to cooperate and make contributions with a sense of service. They act with a strict reciprocity but sometimes also with generosity and gratuity.

The business firm as a community of persons

A more comprehensive view is to understand the identity of a business firm as a *community of persons* who coordinate their efforts and cooperate through an organization for a shared purpose of producing certain goods and services, and simultaneously achieving their particular goals.

A community is generally understood as an *enduring unity* of persons involved in a common action for a shared purpose, although personal motivations can be different. It is worth noting that a community is much more than a set of people interacting for a common purpose, such as a group of people who meet in an organized trip. Building a community needs an enduring unity, a common action and a shared purpose. A family, a neighborhood or a company has enduring unity. They share purpose and collaborate in some way in common actions; so they are communities, although the degree of unity might range from strong to weak.

A community of persons not only emphasizes the idea that shared purpose and collaborative action exist with an enduring unity, but also that a business enterprise is a real entity, something more than the sum of the individuals who form it. It is a real entity, but not an impersonal collective, where persons practically disappear, nor a "living organism," where individuals fully depend on their environment. On the contrary, a business firm depends completely on the individuals of which it is composed, and on the relationships and bonds between them. Thus, seeing a business enterprise as a community of persons provides a comprehensive identity and a guide for a correct understanding of the business firm and of its management.

There are corporations, however, that seem more like impersonal organizations than communities of persons. This is often a result of the particular vision of those who design or manage these corporations, but is not consistent with the demands of the human reality of the business firm. Business firms require material resources, including raw material, information, technology and financial funds, but all of these resources are nothing without people, the entrepreneur, managers, workers, and also those people who make business activity possible: suppliers, clients, customers and so on.

Last but not least is our affirmation that business enterprises are *communities of persons*, which is more explicit than "human community". In this way, we are stressing that people are central in business enterprise, and in managing a business enterprise one should not forget that one is dealing with free and autonomous individuals who voluntarily undertake a corporate activity working together with others to satisfy both individual and common goals; not to be forgotten either is that people have dignity and are continuously open to human flourishing, including when they are working in a firm.

Power and the common good

Within the business firm different people have some type of power, understanding power here as the relationship between two persons or groups, in which one side is getting the other to do what the former wants, and also as the ability to influence the behavior of others. According to an old distinction, there are five sources of power: legitimate, reward, coercive, referent and expert.[17] Managers can have all these types of power, or some of them.

Legitimate power of managers comes from the formal position or role the manager has in the company. Managers generally also have *reward power*, inasmuch as they have the power to control the allocation of pay raises, bonuses, days off, acts of recognition and awards. On the other hand, they have *coercive power* which includes several forms of intimidation of employees through reprimands or punishments, which can reach extremes involving demotion or even the loss of a job. The manager can also have *referent power*, which is managerial power gained as a result of workers seeing the manager as a role model for their work, finding attraction in how the manager works or how he or she uses power or deals with people. *Expert power* stems from the prestige of the manager in a specific area of business, which generates trust and willingness of employees to cooperate and to follow the manager due to his or her expertise and experience.

Whatever the type may be, managers have power which can be used to serve others and to contribute to the common good of the business firm and, ultimately, to the common good of society. However, in business, as in any other society, power can be used selfishly, seeking to gain or retain power at any cost. Those who use power in such a way are often referred to *The Prince* by Niccolò Machiavelli as an illustrative example of how to act to retain power, and how to set aside the morality of the means to achieve this goal. In the 16th century, Machiavelli was an advisor to the prince who ruled the city of Florence, Italy. He gave guidance on how to retain power, suggesting that the prince should be willing to act morally or immorally, depending on the circumstances. This latter type of action includes the occasional need for the exercise of brute force, deceit and so on. Another work often cited as a reference for "successful managers" is *The Art of War*, written by Chinese general Sun Tzu, in the 6th century BC. Although it is about military strategy, its ideas have been said to be also useful to managers. They are based on being aware of and acting on the strengths and weaknesses of both the manager's organization and those of the enemy. Morality and a sense of responsibility are absent in this work.

One of the most repeated claims, however, is that power entails responsibility. The ethical justification of power is not to use it only to retain power, or for personal gains, or to favor one group of people over others without equity. Proper use of power demands acting with justice, respecting people's rights, and serving the common good of the community over particular interests. This is a great challenge for managers.

Responsibility in managerial power does not only concern avoiding unjust use of power. Managerial power can also be misused by acting with negligence, or without the due diligence required by this power, or by employing power in a useless manner. *Negligence* can be found, for instance, in managers who are not aware of the environment – its threats and opportunities – in matters related to their work, or not reasonably foreseeing the future. Power employed in a useless manner is, for instance, using it only for vanity and not for the best interests of the company.

A blatant misuse of managerial power is what is generally termed *opportunism*. Managers have a certain control of ordinary activities in business firms, and can find opportunities which permit them to make "easy money" or to take advantage of their position for personal gains. They act with opportunism when they consciously take selfish advantage of circumstances through certain policies or practices, and disregard ethical principles.

The risk of managerial *opportunistic behavior*, in which managers can take advantage of their control of business and against shareholder interests, was given great consideration in Agency Theory. This theory proposes various mechanisms to align the interests of the agent (employee) with those of the principal (employer). For example, when stockholders (the principal) hire top executives of corporations (agents), the former can try to align the latter with their interests through payment of huge economic compensations, through stock options, piece rates/commissions, profit sharing, efficiency wages and so on. Incentives to align management with stockholder interests may include, for instance, holding shares, profit sharing and wages related to efficiency on the one hand, and a fear of being fired on the other.

These measures can help prevent opportunistic behavior of senior managers or a CEO, but not those who can use their power against the best interest of the company in the long-term, since their economic compensation is often connected to stock price or to other short-term criteria which are not always linked to genuinely good long-term performance.

Remuneration of managers, and particularly the CEO and senior managers, ought to respond to criteria of distributive justice and foster their contribution to the common good. However, this is not always the reality. In recent years the remuneration and compensation of the CEO, especially in large companies, has come under the spotlight of debate. While some criticism made may be due to envy, much may be justified. We will examine this next.

CEO compensation

Applying Agency Theory has contributed to increased CEO remuneration and this compensation has been huge in more than a few cases. In many countries, such as the USA, the setting of CEO compensation falls under the responsibility of the board of directors, but the same CEO or management consultants can also be involved in the process. Astronomic remuneration packages are not infrequently used to tempt a high-profile CEO from outside the company, often with little knowledge about the business and ignorant of the company's culture or its people, perhaps including multi-year contracts that guarantee their compensation, regardless of performance. According to Bill George,[18] the latter is the result of a failure of boards to develop their future CEOs internally. These huge compensations, especially when not connected to real performance, are an outrage to the public, and even to *minority shareholders*.

Inappropriate senior management compensation can erode employee trust and have a negative influence on motivation and work morale. Bill George[19] suggested two criteria for CEO compensation which seem quite reasonable in terms of both ethics and efficiency. The first is to arrange an executive compensation directly tied to the company's long-term objectives and based on building the firm's economic value, not on its stock price. He believes that "the best compensation programs tie up half of the executives' compensation for the duration of their tenure, so they cannot cash in when the company's stock peaks. These programs are based on a mix of short-term and long-term incentives so that no one objective can be pursued to the detriment of the firm's interests". The second criterion is internal equity, which should be given equal weighting so that gaps between CEOs and their subordinates are narrowed, and it is the team that is rewarded for the company's success. This is different from taking only one benchmark group – CEOs of other companies, for instance, who can be easily manipulated – to determine the CEO compensation.

MANAGING PEOPLE'S WORK WITHIN THE BUSINESS FIRM

Human work expresses the human condition. In contrast to animals, humans, rather than adapting themselves to the environment, dominate it and introduce changes through their work, to make it more suitable for proper human life. In a sense, animals also work and produce related to their survival or for the sake of their offspring. In some cases you can even find organized forms of work, as with ants and honey bees. But these are mechanical and repetitive tasks, with no innovation at all. Nowadays, honey bees do the same work, as they did in the Ancient Roman times of Pliny the Elder's *Natural History*. Human work is intentional and reflective, done for a conscious goal, and often creative and innovative. These and all other characteristics of the person should be taken into account in organizing and managing work within the business firm.

Human work brings about external outcomes or products (goods and services), which can have a certain economic value. Within a business firm, it is obviously expected that managers' and employees' work contributes to the goals of the firm and ultimately to the bottom line. Workers receive wages, compensation and other rewards more or less related to their results. However, work also has internal effects, which sometimes can become even more important than those which are external. Internal effects include physical and psychological factors (tiredness, stress, satisfaction, psychological tension, etc.), operative learning in performing the activity, and cognitive and moral learning derived from the perception of the meaning of the work and its consistency with ethical values, and in particular how the work carried out may serve or indeed harm or damage people.

In other words, when someone works, he or she is transforming the environment by making products, but at the same time is perfecting (or eroding) him or herself. Work has both an *objective* (external) meaning and a *subjective* or internal meaning related with the person of the worker, bringing about both external and internal effects which are good for the worker. Both external and internal effects are related to motivations, a familiar topic in management, as we will consider below.

Communicating and motivating

Managers depend on the work of other people to achieve personal and corporate goals. This requires effective communication and being able to properly motivate those collaborating with them.

Communication can create understanding and help to avoid mix-ups or, on the contrary, can bring about misunderstanding and confusion. Effective communication requires adequate techniques regarding communication processes, communication channels and communication relationships. But beyond these techniques, respect for people requires truthfulness, that is, true information and transparency in the disclosure of information, not only that which is necessary to perform work but also that which people have the right to know. Avoiding lies and providing sufficient information also have consequences for efficient management. Lies and opacity create distrust and false rumors, with the risk of jeopardizing leadership and results.

Motivating people is to influence behavior and more specifically what can be called "internal driving forces" or motivations for working – in more general terms, for acting – which are related to goals achievable through the work. Motivation and competence are often viewed as key performance factors.[20] One relevant type of motive in the work context is the associated remuneration, and there are other external rewards such as prestige, promotion and so on (*extrinsic motives*). Another type of motive derives from the action itself, including learning and satisfaction with the work or working conditions (*intrinsic motives*). A third type concerns the meaning of the work, expressed in terms of service to people's needs, sense of responsibility, contribution to the common good, or any moral commitment (*moral motives*).[21] This latter type of motive is the basis for committed employees, fosters cooperation beyond remuneration and pleasure in one's own work, and is related with the ethical dimension of human work and with human flourishing.

Managers motivate collaborators by appealing to extrinsic motives, through economic incentives, for instance; or by appealing to intrinsic motives, say through an appropriate assignation of tasks and responsibilities and by promoting good working conditions. Moral motives are personal, but managers can also have an influence, as noted (see p. 20), acting as role models.

Participation

Participation within a company refers to the act of participating as a conscious and free being in its activity. Participation is taking part in a business firm's activity not as passive receptors of orders but as active persons who feel part of the whole and want to have a voice in organizational life and especially in those aspects of it which affect their lives and activities. Participation refers to taking part in the decision-making process in some way. It can also include sharing profits. A high level of participation includes direct employee ownership of the company.

The notion of participation recognizes human cognitive capacities, freedom and the fact of being in a community, where persons take part in different ways. Participation is an ethical requirement, associated with human freedom and autonomy. This requirement does not entail, however, any particular model. It can be applied in many different ways and degrees, depending on the circumstances, but should always include treating the ideas and suggestions of employees with consideration and respect, and even providing appropriate information and training which permits them to have a better understanding of the company and skills to make their participation more effective.

Participative (or participatory) management tries to apply the idea of participation in managerial decision-making by the involvement of employees and other stakeholders in different ways. The lowest degree of participation is receiving accurate and relevant information about the company and in turn being asked to express their opinions and views on a problem and possible solutions. This elemental participative management, introduced as early as the 1920s, encourages workers to voice their opinions especially in matters closely related to their working conditions, including health and safety, providing suggestions for improvements in their tasks, setting operative goals, determining work schedules and so on. In that decade, Mary Parker Follett, a celebrated pioneer of management, strongly suggested changing "giving orders" for "participation"; and acting through "power with" workers rather than exercising "power over" them.[22]

Higher degrees of participation in the decision-making process include input on the definition of the problem and consulting on generating and proposing alternative courses of action to solve it, and the highest is taking part in the decision, that is, co-deciding what to do. Co-decisions by managers and their co-workers are rare, since senior managers commonly retain their authority in making the final decision. However, in some decisions senior managers may also make decisions together with their collaborators.

Participation does not mean the absence of authority or weakness of character. Nor does reasonable participation require that every decision-making process within the organization should be participative. Participation refers not to trivial matters, but to those matters that really affect people's activities or lives, or to whatever seems reasonably appropriate under the circumstances of each situation. Participation requires responsible people and a willingness to decide not only in line with one's own legitimate interests or the interests of one party, but also, and above all, for the common good of the organization.

In the last two decades participative management has been increasingly proposed, backed by the argument that it can contribute to efficiency by aiding the adaptation of the organization to new technologies, markets, challenges and the dizzying rate of change itself, and some specific techniques have been proposed for this. Self-managed teams, quality circles, or committees concerning work–life balance are some of these forms. Others are soliciting survey feedback, allowing employees to take part in making decisions and empowering them to make certain types of decisions. However, some recent practices related to downsizing or outsourcing show a failure of participative management.[23]

It is worth noting that participation is basically a generic concept, and not every tool of participative management is an ethical requirement. Decisions on this latter point need a wise evaluation of what might be best in each circumstance.

Organizational structures

Companies need strategies and objectives within the framework of their mission and an organizational structure to achieve them. The latter consists of the distribution of authority and formal lines of communication, decision-making power, responsibilities and task allocation, job design, and coordination and supervision.

Managers focus on organizational structures which favor efficiency and should also focus on the role of these structures in favoring personal growth, or perhaps in hampering it. What is first of all required is to avoid organizational structures which favor misbehavior. One of the triggers for employee misbehavior can stem from the *organizational rewards system*. It occurs, for instance, when pressure for results is not accompanied by clear and efficient norms prohibiting bribes or frauds. If managers are not aware of this in designing rewards systems, unintentionally they may incentivize undesirable actions. Another important element which can foster or impede personal growth is the design and execution of *performance appraisal*, where the job performance is evaluated, generally by the corresponding manager or supervisor. If performance evaluation only occurs in terms of business goals, without paying attention to integrity, values, concern for service and so on, it can incentivize amoral behavior and a mindset in which only the economic counts and not people.

A crucial cornerstone in the organizational structure is the extent to which employees enjoy freedom to organize their work as much as possible, take the initiative and make decisions in harmony with the achievement of the organization's more general goals. This is a requirement of a principle of social ethics known as the *principle of subsidiarity*,[24] which establishes that a larger and higher-ranking body should not exercise functions that could be efficiently carried out by a smaller and lesser body; rather, the former should support the latter by aiding it in the coordination of its activities with those of the larger community, always under the guidance of the common good of the community. This principle respects human freedom and diversity, and at the same time makes possible the contributions of people's talents without submitting everybody to a grey uniformity.

From the beginning of the 20th century to post-World War II, organizational structure was strongly bureaucratic, with scarce respect for the principle of subsidiarity. It was characterized by a clear hierarchical reporting structure through a tightly-knit chain-of-command and a rigid set of rules, standards and procedures associated with highly specialized jobs and functional departments. People in the organization were a cog in a machine, no matter their rung on the ladder of the hierarchy. People's autonomy, creativity and initiative were quite limited, and the idea of personal growth was nonexistent. This was presented as the "one best way" to be effective. However, this dominant logic to do a job gradually changed, and now to a greater extent organizational structures tend to promote personal responsibility, creativity and innovation.

These new organizational tendencies are not only closer to the principle of subsidiarity, but can also bring about more efficiency. Many new organizational structures have flexibility and take personal initiative and responsibility seriously, and in doing so favor agile manufacturing and provide adaptability to change. This is important in a context of global competition and fast changes, where companies need the ability to be efficient now and adaptable to changes which may be nearby.

BUILDING UP A PERSON-CENTERED CORPORATE CULTURE

Considering the centrality of the person within organizations also has its expression in the organizational culture and includes shared beliefs, ideas and values, along with different artifacts, practices and behavioral styles.

The view of the person presented above, along with his or her dignity, rights and openness to human flourishing, are central in a person-centered culture. This culture involves justice, with its related values, and intelligent love, including care and friendly-based recipro-city, as explained above.

Among the factors usually mentioned in relation to corporate culture, some seem particularly relevant to building a person-centered culture. These include the following:

(1)   Recruiting, selecting and promoting people who are not only competent but who have a human quality.
This requires paying special attention to the values and virtues of people in the recruitment, selection and promotion process. Human quality is particularly important in the CEO and senior management, since these act as role models and their leadership is generally recog-nized as crucial to the development of corporate cultures. Training of employees can be another important element in promoting a person-centered culture.

(2)   Consistency of the centrality of the person in corporate missions, policies and decision-making.
A well-defined corporate mission, as well as a corporate vision and values statements which express a real service to people, consti-tute a message both inside and outside the business firm. These can contribute to creating a person-centered culture if they are accom-panied by a serious commitment to implementing such statements and if such intentions are put into practice. It is especially relevant to develop corporate policies consistent with person-related values and to integrate these values into decision-making at all levels of the company. Otherwise mission, vision and values remain ineffec-tive and people understand that such corporate statements are only a matter of rhetoric.

(3)   Developing person-oriented organizational and power structures.
As noted, organizational structures can contribute to both good and bad behaviors. Organizational structure can also indicate that people-oriented contributions are valued more than selfish behaviors, while power structures can indicate a sense of service and consideration for people in those who have a great amount of power or influence within the business firm.

(4)   Designing and operating with fair and caring control systems.
Control systems include financial, quality and reward systems. Fairness entails both the measuring and the distribution within the organiza-tion. There are a number of managerial practices which require an evaluative process. This is the case of performance appraisal or in the selection and promotion of people.

Fairness in performance appraisal requires avoiding biased attitudes or evaluating without accurate and true information. This should be the case, for instance, in analyzing the employee's successes and failures, and his or her achievement of goals and objectives. Care and intelligent love, along with concern for the common good, entail giving accurate feedback to employees about their respective strengths and weaknesses, in recommending appropriate training or in creating expectations of promotion or rewards.

(5) Acting with justice and intelligent love in dealing with people.
This includes both formal and informal treatment. As noted above, respect is the basic requirement for dealing with people. First of all, this demands, avoiding blatant injustice and indifference in relations with people, and respect for human dignity and rights. Particularly significant in the business context are avoiding unfair discrimination, humiliation, injury and offence, sexual and psychological harassment, and other practices which are recognizable as being contrary to human dignity, such as a lack of respect for religious freedom and diversity.

Apart from human rights, justice requires equality in exchanges, honoring contracts and keeping one's word. Justice can also include equity in applying criteria in the remuneration and in evaluation processes. Justice requires appropriateness in recognizing merits, and taking care not to falsely appropriate what has been done by another.

(6) Considering the centrality of the person in ceremonies and events, stories and symbols.
All of these elements can show employees what behavior is desirable and valued by senior management, and motivate and foster a sense of mutual esteem, service and cooperation. The events a company has, stories on company "heroes" and how crises or difficult situations were overcome in the past, along with the language and symbols used, or taking care of company facilities can also build up a person-centered culture if all of these express respect, concern and mutual esteem and a sense of cooperation and commitment to the common goals of the business firm.

EXECUTIVE SUMMARY

A correct understanding of the human being means dealing with people in a proper way, considering that they are individuals with a conscience, freedom and numerous possibilities for self-realization; and avoiding seeing them as mere resources or a simple means for profit. Humanistic management is about recognizing what people are, treating them accordingly and fostering their development.

Person is taken here as a synonym for human being, a living being endowed with emotions, rationality and freedom. The notion of *person* encompasses dignity and a sense of uniqueness. Persons have rationality which includes self-possession, intimacy and openness to transcendence. Freedom provides the capacity for making conscious and self-determined decisions and to act with autonomy. As a consequence persons are responsible and accountable for actions they perform or omit with deliberation and freedom. Genetic inheritance and culture have an influence on human behavior but individual behavior is not completely conditioned by such factors. Human beings are free and, therefore, owners of their actions, except maybe in some extreme conditions. The human being is a relational and social being, with the capacity to establish relationships with other personal beings and to enrich their character and personhood through such relations. Virtues contribute to human flourishing, in which a true neighborly love is crucial. Human features such as rationality, free will and the inner self of each person make human dignity quite evident.

Management is about people, and the previous consideration leads to the centrality of the person in management. This has at least four consequences. The first concerns a *human quality* in dealing with people. Managing people can entail different degrees of human quality. We distinguish five levels: (1) mistreatment, which entails a blatant injustice, (2) indifference toward persons, which is disrespect for people, (3) respectful treatment, which is that required by justice, (4) concern for people's interests, or care, and (5) a friendship-based reciprocity, in which a great consideration of the person exists; it is expressed in terms of mutual esteem among people, and a willingness for cooperation and service toward the common good. These latter two points go beyond justice, showing an intelligent love.

The second consequence is about seeing the business firm as a *community of persons* with a specific mission. Thus, business is more than a set of contracts in a system of interests. The business firm is made up of people bonded together by the common purpose of producing certain goods and services, and simultaneously achieving their particular goals. In a community like the business firm, there are different types of power but in any case power requires responsibility and its legitimacy comes from serving the common good. Some CEO compensation is an abuse of power.

The third consequence regards people's work and *work organization* within the business firm. Communication based on truthfulness and transparency is necessary for a sound organization of work. Motivation can foster acting and developing the noblest inclination of the human being and human development. But what is really crucial in considering the centrality of the person and in favoring personal growth is the organizational structure.

The fourth consequence of the centrality of the person is building up a *corporate culture* which can become a person-centered culture. Such a culture can be promoted by (1) recruiting, selecting and promoting people who are not only competent but who have a human quality, (2) consistently ensuring the centrality of the person in corporate missions and values, strategies, policies and decision-making, (3) developing person-oriented organizational and power structures, (4) designing and operating with fair and caring control systems, (5) acting with justice and intelligent love in dealing with people, and (6) considering the centrality of the person in ceremonies and events, stories and symbols.

CHAPTER 5

MANAGING CORPORATE RESPONSIBILITY AND SUSTAINABILITY

… those companies that devote themselves to maximizing share-holder value as their primary purpose will ultimately fail to do so in the long run. The best path to long term growth in shareholder value comes from having a well-articulated mission that employees are willing to commit to, a consistently practiced set of values, and a clear strategy that is adaptable to changing business conditions.[1]

WILLIAM W. GEORGE (b. 1942)
Former Chairman and CEO of Medtronic

William W. George was CEO of Medtronic between 1992 and 2001, and later Chair of this high-tech medical company. A company which produces electronic devices to alleviate pain, among others, was indeed a mission-driven company and values-centered organization and one with an adaptable business strategy. It showed a considerable and sustained growth, at least during George's tenure as CEO. It reported 64 consecutive quarters of increasing revenues and earnings. The introductory words of this chapter belong to his keynote address on receiving the Distinguished Executive of the Year Award at the Academy of Management's annual conference in 2001. After his retirement, George taught at IMD, Switzerland, at Yale School of Management and at Harvard Business School, and wrote several books. He explained that he chose Medtronic, after years of professional life, because he found there all he wanted: values, passion and the opportunity to help people suffering from chronic disease.[2]

Many business enterprises, like Medtronic, make good products, while still making profits and maintaining an increasing share price over very long periods of time. Alleviating pain is clearly a service to people, but other business products also provide a service to people in some way. *Service and profits* are closely related. But what comes first? For many decades the mainstream idea about the purpose of business has been that the supreme goal of the firm is the maximization of shareholder value. Other goals of business are not denied, but they should be subordinated to the maximization of shareholder value. Today, this idea is being seriously questioned by many who have proposed alternative views of the purpose of the firm in society.

The view of the purpose of firm in society is a crucial aspect of the ethos of management (see pp. 8–11), which conditions the ultimate orientation of business management and how the responsibility of business in society is understood. It is also related to how business can contribute to sustainability. In this chapter, we will discuss the purpose of the firm in society, and how to manage corporate responsibility and sustainability. As an introduction we present a short view on how ideas about corporate social responsibility and sustainability have been developed over time.

CORPORATE RESPONSIBILITY AND SUSTAINABILITY: AN HISTORICAL OVERVIEW

From the time of the *Industrial Revolution* (or perhaps even earlier) the prevailing opinion was that business responsibility was exclusively economic in nature, and without any social dimension. Nevertheless, there have been entrepreneurs and managers that have shown a laudable sense of responsibility especially toward their employees. They believed that business entails moral and social responsibility. It is also worth remembering that such currently well-known corporations as HP, IBM and Johnson & Johnson were built on strong ethical values.

The separation between ownership and managerial *control* from the early decades of the 20th century also raised questions as to the social responsibilities of managers and of companies. As corporate executives became ever more powerful, the idea that *power requires responsibility* became more widespread.

Another fact which favored the voluntary acceptance of social responsibility of business was increasing governmental regulation and the response to this of business. After the Stock Market Crash of 1929 Roosevelt's New Deal brought greater governmental intervention in the US economy and led to the regulation of key areas of business. In Europe, too, there was increased government intervention in the economy, and this became more patent after World War II. Business strongly felt it was desirable to *avoid new regulations*, and realized that if companies did not freely accept that they had social responsibilities, the government would force them to do so in maybe less favorable terms.

The idea that accepting social responsibilities was a matter of *enlightened self-interest* progressively spread. In the long run, there were advantages to be gained by taking the social responsibility of business seriously. This argument gave rise to a movement in favor of corporate social responsibility, which reached a peak in the 1950s and 1960s. The movement in favor of corporate social responsibility won numerous supporters, and many top executives proclaimed that, besides their economic responsibility toward their shareholders, companies also had social responsibilities toward their employees and other social groups, and toward the environment.

In addition, from the 1960s, a wave of protests against big business made it clear that a new approach to social responsibility was needed as a matter of *risk avoidance*. This decade was marked by a loud outcry against abuses in product information and safety, protests against racial discrimination, demands for protection of workers' health, angry public reactions against certain business practices and the use of bribery in foreign countries.

In the 1970s the *civil rights movement* and the social reaction to large-scale corporate bribes to foreign politicians, such as the Lockheed scandal which provoked the resignation of the Japanese Prime Minister, demanded more ethical behaviour from both business corporations and governments. Throughout this time, both academics and practitioners have shown a significant and growing interest in business ethics. From the 1980s and into the 1990s, many corporations introduced a corporate code of conduct, corporate values, a corporate mission statement with values, or similar statements, which only a few companies had previously possessed.

In addition, we have seen serious industrial accidents, such as that of Bhopal, India in 1984, with thousands of victims, which many thought could have been avoided, and problems with nuclear plants in Chernobyl (1986) in the former Soviet Republic and, for very different reasons, the troubles with the Japanese tsunami disaster in 2011. There was also a fair amount of criticism of the capitalist system as a whole and of corporate executives in particular. Companies were required to defend themselves and to prevent potential risks.

In the late 20th century a new view of corporate responsibility emerged from the concept of *stakeholder management*. According to this type of management, the manager bears responsibility toward all stakeholders or constituencies of the firm, including shareholders, employees, suppliers, customers and, depending on the specific situation, possibly others, including the local community. Stakeholder management requires business ethics, since it permits and even demands the integration of ethical theory, as we will see below.

In the 1990s an increasing interest in good practices of *corporate governance* emerged and, through a number of corporate governance reports, the idea of social responsibility began to be included in questions on how a corporation is directed, administered or controlled. The requirement for *transparency* and *accountability* was strongly emphasized.

At the turn of the 21st century there was a new impulse for corporate social responsibility, although this was often restricted to social activities carried out or supported by companies. This period saw the contribution of corporate responsibility, and its external visibility through corporate auditing and reporting, as being mainly relevant for purposes of *corporate reputation*. Corporate reports began to include topics such as corporate governance, environmental stewardship, health and safety, social affairs and diversity, supplier relations, sustainable innovation, consumer responsibility, climate change and corporate philanthropy. Rankings, certifications and awards contributed to this focus. At the same time, a new demand for business ethics and corporate responsibility was emerging in response to a series of well-known cases involving business scandals and political and business corruption, such as Enron, Parmalat and Madoff, among many others. National, supranational or international organizations, including the United Nations, the Organization for Economic Cooperation and Development (OECD) and the European Union, became stronger in their encouragement of corporate responsibility, and significant international standards for corporate responsibility, accountability and sustainability appeared. Among them the *UN Global Compact*, already mentioned (see p. 84), which includes ten principles taken from its international conventions or declarations (human rights, labor rights, environmental protection and anti-corruption); the *Global Reporting Initiative* (GRI), a network-based organization that produces a comprehensive sustainability reporting framework that is widely used globally; and the *Guidance on Social Responsibility ISO 26000*, provided by the International Organization for Standardization in order to encourage the implementation of best practice in social responsibility worldwide.[3] The global financial crisis which broke in 2007 brought more demands, these mainly addressed at the regulation and monitoring of financial institutions.

From a different perspective, the notion of *sustainability* has come to have a great impact on corporate responsibility. There is a still-growing concern about pollution, the accelerating depletion of natural resources and other threats to the planet. In 1987 the *Brundtland Commission Report*, promoted by the United Nations, defined sustainable development as that which "meets the needs of the present without compromising the ability of future generations to meet their own needs".[4] Although sustainable development focussed initially only on the natural environment, it later acquired a wider meaning, including interest in people and in the social environment and a greater consideration for future generations to come. Many corporate annual reports now refer to sustainability and consider a triple bottom line: economic, social and environmental.

This short historical overview may help in understanding the situation as we find it now, and the current motives for responsible corporate behavior.

MOTIVES FOR RESPONSIBLE CORPORATE BEHAVIOR

Although in a strict sense only people bear responsibility for their actions, certain responsibility can be attributed to "corporate behavior" in which many cooperate, each one with his or her personal responsibility.

Four types of motives for responsible corporate behavior can be distinguished. Three of these come from pressures[5]: from (1) primary stakeholders, (2) governments and institutions and (3) social groups, including mass media, non-governmental organizations (NGOs), civic associations and corporate activists. From a different perspective, there are also moral motivations (Figure 5.1).

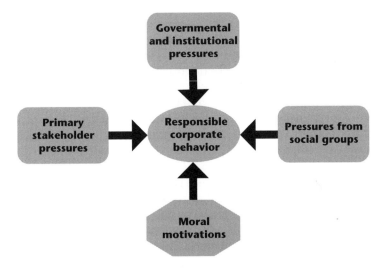

FIGURE 5.1   Motivations for responsible corporate behavior

Primary stakeholder pressures

Stakeholders are people affected by or who can affect the activity of the firm. Among these, primary stakeholders are constituencies of the firm without whom the firm cannot operate. This group generally includes shareholders, employees, customers, suppliers and the local community. All of these can exert pressure in some way for responsible corporate behavior.

Shareholders want a return on their investment. Presenting shareholders as people without any moral or social responsibility, whose only concern is money, is a questionable generalization, even more so if the objective is short-term money. This may be tempting, but many investors are interested in sustainable company growth, with the priority being the long-term return, with only a reasonable short-term return sought. These aims require paying attention to other stakeholder interests, apart from those of the shareholders.[6]

In addition, some investors are aware of the moral, social and cultural dimension of every investment, since for good or bad, investing in a company is a way of cooperating with its activity. This can be especially significant in small and medium-sized companies, but also applies to investment in large companies. Some people refuse to invest in business with questionable records on social responsibility, and instead invest in *ethical funds* which exclude some types of industries. Others seek to invest in socially screened equities. In line with this, there is now a movement, quite active in many countries, which encourages investment in socially responsible companies (ethical funds, social investment funds, etc.). Now there are indexes for responsible social investments, including the *Dow Jones Sustainability Indexes* which track the financial performance of the leading sustainability-driven companies worldwide. The responsible investment movement puts an increasing pressure on companies to provide information about how they manage ethics and corporate social responsibility. In addition, in some countries *shareholder activism* exists with the aim of pressing for corporate resolutions on ethical, social and environmental issues.

Employees can exert pressure for responsible corporate behaviors in several ways. Responsible companies can attract talented managers and employees, and the opposite will also be true. Some studies show that corporate responsibility can have an influence on employee decisions about where to work,[7] while morally sensitive managers and employees will leave their company because of a disagreement about how the firm assumes responsibilities on ethical matters. The motivation and willingness of employees to cooperate can be favored by giving them fair treatment and applying responsible labor standards, while a lack of consideration, poor working conditions (wages, health and safety, etc.) and unfair treatment can erode the morale and motivation of employees.

Consumers and clients have purchasing power which they can use against companies showing a lack of responsibility. Consumers are increasingly engaged in *consumer associations* and this gives them greater possibilities to act both in favor of responsible companies and against irresponsible ones. In addition, some customers will relate their purchasing decisions to their perception of a company's responsibility practices. Potential consumers can also pressure companies to change irresponsible practices such as advertising campaigns which include offensive elements or sponsorship of TV programs or other activities which are seen as irresponsible or disrespectful in terms of ethical values.

Suppliers, although generally with less power than other stakeholders, can also pressure companies. Suppliers, sometimes through alliances or with the support of Non-Governmental Organizations (NGOs), can require responsible behavior in negotiation and fair trade conditions, without abusing their power (this can be the case in other situations, e.g., large stores squeezing small suppliers, big clients in international trade abusing the needs of small businesses in emerging economies). Such settlements allow the suppliers to meet their commitments, and favors their possibility of continuing in business.

The local community where a company operates is often another primary stakeholder that can affect its business activity in both a positive and negative manner. The local community will protest about negative impacts on the population (noise, air or water pollution). It may also pressure for *corporate community involvement* to solve local problems (e.g., education, social exclusion) or to give support to social activities, including cultural events, sports facilities or support for local sport clubs and so on.

Governmental and institutional pressures

Governments have several means to pressure for responsible corporate behavior. First of all, they act through laws and regulations which cover a wide variety of requirements, including labor and civil rights, consumerism and the environment.

Apart from these, governments can stimulate social responsibility through campaigns promoting some aspect of responsibility (e.g., safety conditions, no discrimination), by offering tax incentives or rewards or developing specific policies, providing support agencies, financing research and conferences and so on. *Partnerships* between governmental agencies and private corporations to work on social issues are also possible.

National or international organizations also apply pressure or otherwise try to facilitate responsible and sustainable behavior. This is the case of the UN Global Compact, the *Guidance on Social Responsibility* ISO 26000 and the GRI sustainability reporting framework.

Pressures from social groups

Apart from local community pressures, business firms, especially large corporations, are often under scrutiny from certain *NGOs* and *social activists*, and also from different institutions that can take legal proceedings against companies on issues such as ecology, human rights, consumerism and transparency. *Mass media* can often pressure business either directly or by echoing NGOs, social activists, or other social or moral voices.

Companies are coming under increasing pressure from some of these social agents to take responsibility not only for their own activities but also for their supply chains, which sometimes includes shops or factories with very poor working conditions (sweatshops).

In a different sense, society also pressures for responsible corporate behavior through *rankings* of socially responsible companies and by giving awards. Being in the "top ten" can be a great incentive for some companies to enhance their reputation.

Moral motivations

As noted in the historical overview, pressures from different fronts have had a great influence in promoting corporate behavior. But is responsible corporate behavior only a matter of pressure triggered by corporate reputation factors? A cynic might answer, yes, of course; and often may be right. Pressures should be considered, but are they the only reason for companies to act with responsibility? In addition, we might also ask: do pressures provide an appropriate framework for true corporate responsibility? Might pressures not, on occasion, involve demagogy?

There are undoubtedly moral motives for managing business and society relationships responsibly. These motives come from the consideration of the obligation of the business firm, as of any other social group or institution, to contribute to the common good of society, being a *good corporate citizen*.

People with low ethical sensibility might not be highly interested in the moral motives, but will recognize pressures, and probably also the influence of responsible behavior on the bottom line in the medium and long term. The result here may involve good initiatives from the firms in question, but there is a lack of sound ethical criteria for managing toward the common good of society. Everything depends on the moral quality of the pressures. This moral quality is provided by ethics.

In considering what responsible corporate behavior is, a deeper and more basic problem arises, related to the purpose of the firm in society.

Believing that the purpose of the firm is exclusively to make profits or to maximize its share value leads to a different view of corporate responsibility than that of accepting that profits are necessary but that the firm is much more than an instrument for making profits. This is the next topic we will discuss.

THE PURPOSE OF THE BUSINESS FIRM IN SOCIETY

The *purpose of business* refers to the role of business in society and its social and ethical justification. This is different from the *subjective motive* for undertaking or managing a business, which for many is making money. The purpose of the firm as an institution within society is more complex than this subjective motivation. To understand the purpose of business, we need to recognize that business benefits several groups of people, and that various factors must be present for a business to survive. However, it is obvious that making profits has an important function in business activity, but it is an instrumental role.

The instrumental role of profits

Profit is a measure of business activity provided by the market. It is related to the acceptation of products and the satisfaction of customers, business efficiency and competitive conditions. Profit is indicative of the economic performance of the business, but is not sufficient to guarantee that everything has been done correctly. One can obtain profits at the cost of exploitation of workers or the disrespectful treatment of other stakeholders. Profit may also be obtained without any consideration for the environment.

Companies must generate *sufficient profit*, or at least be in a position to generate sufficient profit in the near future. Otherwise they will not be viable because they will burn through their owners' assets and will have to be shut down. Profits ensure the company's long-term survival and, if possible, reasonable growth.

Even those organizations termed non-profit (e.g., a non-profit hospital or a school managed by parents), meaning that profit is out of their mission, need a sense of profitability; at least to balance expenditure and income, even though the latter may include donations. But for ordinary businesses there is no way to survive without profits.

Thus, profits have an instrumental role in a business firm. Accepting that business is a community of people which includes providers of capital, profits should be taken as being instrumental; important indeed, but instrumental.

Charles Handy, one of the great European thinkers in management, affirmed: "Profits are the lifeblood of any business, but life consists of more than keeping the blood flowing; otherwise, it would not be worth living. As more corporations realize this truth, they will become increasingly interested in enriching the lives of the people who work in them. In time, the laws governing corporations will change to reflect the new reality. First, however, we need a language to explain this new theory – a language of community and citizenship, not of property."[8]

Going back to the purpose of the business firm in society, two mainstream approaches are generally considered: the shareholder and the stakeholder approaches. We will discuss these and afterwards introduce a third, which is currently emerging and which takes into consideration some relevant aspects of the first two but adopts a wider perspective: the common good stakeholder approach.

Shareholder approach

One proposal regarding the purpose of the firm is generally known as the shareholder approach. This is the well-known position of Milton Friedman, who summarized his view in a famous article published in the *New York Times Magazine* in 1970, in which he affirmed: "the only one responsibility of business towards the society is the maximization of profits to the shareholders, within the legal framework and the ethical custom of the country".[9] This entails a particular ethos, in which society is seen as built by a social contract among individuals, and the exclusive function of business is creating wealth. The business relationship with society only regards compliance with the law and the basic "rules of the game" of the free market economy.[10] Property rights are seen as practically absolute and the only obligation of managers consists of their fiduciary duties to shareholders, apart from the compliance with the law and some other elemental rules, as noted. From this approach, if law is quite permissive with labor rights, the environment or whatever, companies do not have any responsibility for these matters at all, even if they are disrespectful to persons or pollute or destroy the environment. In the shareholder approach, profits and share value are not a means but the supreme end. The root of this approach is in making proprietary rights central. Capital is necessary but so too are the people who work and spend an important part of their life working in the firm. Nowadays, within the *knowledge society*, people are often more important in terms of the survival of the firm.

This position can be qualified as *economism*, since economic is the dominant, or even exclusive, view of the firm and its purpose in society. The question which arises is whether business also has a *social function* apart from its undeniable economic function.

In the last third of the 20th century, an expression of economism arose, becoming a new creed in the business world.[11] In this view the role of the manager is exclusively to serve the principal interests. Shareholders are seen as the principal and managers as agents of this principal, and the latter should be aligned with the former through strong incentives – this is formalized by the Agency Theory (see pp. 90–91). In line with this, the rate of return on corporate stock was taken as the measure of a superior performance and managers' remuneration. This introduced the problem of exorbitant compensations to CEOs (see p. 91). In theory, this position does not exclude paying attention to stakeholder interests if this can contribute to the bottom line in the long-term.[12] In practice, however, this approach is commonly applied to maximize short-term share value.

In recent years economism has come under criticism from different perspectives, including its "mechanistic view" of business and society, its questionable ethical foundations and the consequences for the long-term when the only compass to manage a firm is the incentives associated with the short-term considerations of the situation in the market.

Stakeholder approach

As an alternative to this *shareholder approach*, the *stakeholder orientation* or stakeholder management has been proposed.[13] According to this proposal – introduced by R. Edward Freeman[14] in 1984 and refined over the following years – the corporation ought to be managed for the benefit of its stakeholders, including shareholders but also others such as employees, customers, suppliers and local communities. This view holds that the purpose of the firm is to create value for all stakeholders, and not only for shareholders. Consequently, management must act in the interests of the stakeholders, balancing these interests by using some ethical theory. The interest of the corporation to ensure the survival of the firm, safeguarding the long-term stakes of each group, should also be taken into account. The pharmaceutical company Merck, for instance, expresses this position by presenting its corporate mission as: "To provide innovative, distinctive products and services that save and improve lives and satisfy customer needs, to be recognized as a great place to work, and to provide investors with a superior rate of return."[15]

This stakeholder approach is based on accepting stakeholder interests as an ethical duty, a duty which some authors reduce to "legitimate stakeholder interest". It also considers that property rights are not absolute but should be based upon an underlying principle of distributive justice.[16]

There is increasing agreement that focusing on stakeholder interests can contribute to maximizing shareholder value in the long term. In Freeman's words: "to maximize shareholder value over an uncertain time frame, managers ought to pay attention to key stakeholder relationships".[17] In his view, if you consider the long term, Freeman's position converges with that of Friedman.[18]

Even so, stakeholder management seeks to create value not only to shareholders, with a maximum return in the long term, but for all stakeholders. The creation of value for every stakeholder can have a wider sense, and not be restricted to only the economic.[19] It can also include value in terms of satisfaction, learning or development.

The stakeholder orientation is more respectful to persons than the shareholder approach, but it does entail some ethical ambiguities. Among these are the quest for the moral legitimacy of stakeholder interests and how to properly balance interests in conflict. In addition, this approach does not make clear how it contributes to the common good of society, which is more than the sum of individual interests (see pp. 31–32). These limitations lead us to another view, which does not exclude value creation in a broad sense for the stakeholder but, in addition, offers a wider perspective.

Common good stakeholder approach

This approach generally considers the business firm as a community of persons (see pp. 87–91) within society, and not only a system of stakeholder interests. It takes the common good of the firm and its *contribution to the common good* of society at large as the key orientation for corporate governance and management. This generic orientation is made specific, as we will see below, through specific responsibilities. This is compatible with considering responsibilities toward stakeholders[20] but adopts a higher perspective than the pure stakeholder approach.

The ethos of this approach is different from the previous approaches in the consideration of the human being, the business firm and society. Consideration of the human being entails taking human relationability and sociability (see pp. 79–80) into account.

The relationability of human beings includes freedom and autonomy but also the capacity to establish interpersonal bonds. Sociability entails living together united by the willingness to cooperate toward common goals with a sense of community which goes beyond social contracts exclusively based on interests and implicit agreements. Sociability leads to assuming social responsibility for the impact of one's actions – or business activity – on others or on society. From this perspective, society is seen as a set of persons united and forming a real whole, but maintaining their condition as free and autonomous beings. Business is a part of society, not an autonomous sphere along-side society and the State.

It can also be said that the firm is an *intermediate* or *mediating* institution between the individual and global society, together with many other intermediate institutions (family, cultural, religious, sporting, charity, neighbourhood and municipal associations, etc.), which carry out certain mediation and so contribute to the formation of an interpersonal and social nexus and to the social manifestation of the individual identity. Thus, the firm can be considered a mediating institution.[21] This view contrasts with the view of society in which business and the State (mainly government) are two separate spheres, the former oriented to wealth creation and the latter to preventing abuses by companies in their activity through laws and regulations, and to promoting redistribution of wealth through social policies.

An elemental reflection on business in society highlights that business enterprises are born in society, operate within society, use means provided by society and their activity is addressed toward society, in such a way that society receives benefits and sometimes damage from businesses. In addition, business uses material resources from the environment and deposits waste in it. There is no way to isolate business from society, except perhaps for analytical purposes. Business is undoubtedly within society, a part of society. Furthermore, business is a pillar of society by virtue of its specific contributions. These include making products more accessible through efficient manufacturing systems, while trying to respect human rights and the environment, creating wealth and providing channels for profitable investment, providing jobs – where workers gain their livelihood and can grow as people and acquire knowledge and skills, developing new products, technology and processes which can contribute to people's wellbeing, and creating an opportunity for suppliers' activity. These positive contributions do not take away the fact that a few companies make a contribution which is not positive, but what happens is not always what ought to be.

If a business firm is a community of persons and this community is part of a larger community, it is not reasonable to think that a business should be a parasite of society or even a cancer which destroys society – it has to be a party that actively contributes to the wellbeing of society. Thus, the purpose of business in society cannot be other than to contribute to the common good in accordance with its specific activity of providing goods and services at a profit. Furthermore, associated with this goal, business also contributes to the common good in other ways, as we will discuss below.

That the firm serves the common good of society is the fundamental ethical principle for company–society relations and establishes the responsibilities of the firm in society.

HUMAN AND SUSTAINABLE DEVELOPMENT

Human development is understood here as the flourishing of individuals and their respective communities. This human development and the environment where such development takes place are considered in their present situation and in their influence on future generations. The latter is expressed through the idea of sustainable development. Concern for human and sustainable development is actually concern for the common good (see pp. 31–32) understood in its broader sense.

Business contributes to human and sustainable development in different ways, as noted (see p. 113), but its contribution may also be negative. The latter occurs, for instance, in supplying harmful goods or services, creating wealth unfairly, and maintaining jobs and work conditions in which human dignity is not sufficiently respected or human flourishing is prevented. The common good can also be eroded when companies are involved in corruption or an abusive consumption of natural resources, pollution, inappropriate waste disposal, and so on, and by a lack of an appropriate balance between work and private or family life.

Human development

Human development requires, first of all, respect for human rights, avoiding misbehavior, corruption and everything which opposes human development, and promoting whatever will foster such development. Therefore, a responsible company should be organized in such a way that people can improve through their work, or at least their work does not impede such improvement. Corporate activity would lose its *moral legitimacy* if the pursuit of profit or other goals entailed neglecting human rights, manipulating people or degrading their humanity.

Similarly, on the side of consumers, respect for people leads to taking care to avoid manipulating people or to sell products which can erode human development as happens with some hazardous consumer products, violent and sexually explicit video games and unhealthy foods. Business, along with society, can foster responsible and sustainable consumption and encourage the changing of products and processes for other more ecological alternatives. This is the case, for instance, of substituting fuel-inefficient vehicles for others which are more efficient and less polluting.

Sustainable development

Sustainability, from the Latin *sustinere* (*tenere*, to hold; *sus*, up), has the modern meaning of "capable of being continued at a certain level". Since the 1980s, this term has been used in the sense of human sustainability on our planet, in that a sustainable development has to meet the needs of the present without compromising the ability of future generations to meet their own needs. Thus sustainability was initially centered on the natural environment, but has come to be understood in a broader sense by distinguishing three inherent dimensions: economic, social and environmental. The *economic dimension* refers to economic growth which is sustainable over time, the *social dimension* regards justice, harmony and peace, alleviation of poverty and "human ecology", considering the human, social and cultural legacy to later generations, and the *environmental dimension* refers to the use of resources, disposal of waste and pollution in all its forms. This triple dimension of sustainability emphasizes the "Triple P": *People, Planet and Profit*, like a three-legged stool on which sustainability is placed.

Ethics provide the moral foundation of sustainability, which is none other than the common good, seen from the perspective of both current and future generations. Without ethics, sustainability might be a matter of preferences, fashions or pressures. Furthermore, one or other aspect of sustainability could arbitrarily be seen to have primacy over others. Jeffrey Pfeffer,[22] a renowned professor at Stanford University, criticized the current tendency where sustainability is mainly focused on the physical environment, while companies and their management practices profoundly affect the human and social environment as well. He affirmed: "It is not just the natural world that is at risk from harmful business practices. We should care as much about people as we do about polar bears – or the environmental savings from using better milk jugs – and also understand the causes and consequences of how we focus our research and policy attention."[23]

Regarding sustainability, ethics, as in other matters, take human dignity seriously, but this is not in opposition to a greater respect for the natural environment. As the first principle of the *UN Rio Declaration on Environment and Development* affirms: "Human beings are at the centre of concern for sustainable development. They are entitled to a healthy and productive life in harmony with nature." This is a position of *moderate anthropocentrism* (or *steward-anthropocentrism*), in which humans should bear a sense of stewardship for nature. This differs from a *dominative anthropocentrism* where the natural environment is seen as no more than a possession to serve the interests of its owners, without further consideration. From this perspective, nature may be continuously manipulated through technology with no possibility of recovery. In the other extreme we find theories, such as that called *deep ecology*, in which humans are diluted within nature. This falls short in its consideration of the human being. Humans, though part of nature, also transcend it because of their inner self, with its significant spiritual dimension.

That being said, it is time to discuss the contribution of business to the common good and the subsequent duty to manage corporate responsibilities.

RESPONSIBILITIES OF BUSINESS IN SOCIETY

Business can be seen as a corporate actor within society with three different functions (instrumental, integrative and social), and through these dimensions it contributes to human and sustainable development and therefore to the common good. This is the source for the responsibilities of business in society. The business firm has an *instrumental function* for wealth and knowledge creation, an *integrative function* for the stakeholders of the firm, and a *politico-social function* within society at large, with which the business firm interacts and to which it makes some additional contributions. In these three aspects a business firm can contribute to the common good when its activity is driven by promoting – or at least not preventing – human and sustainable development. This requires sustainable wealth and knowledge creation in acting in its instrumental dimension; responsible stakeholder treatment in acting as integrative agent and corporate citizen behavior in its politico-social function (see Figure 5.2). We will discuss these requirements next.

Sustainable creation of wealth and knowledge

Creating wealth, understood in a very broad sense, means generating economic utility to make a profit now, or to improve the company's competitive position so that it will make a profit in the future. One indicator of wealth creation is the *Economic Value Added* (EVA), defined as the difference between sales revenue from ordinary operations and payments made for the purchase or use of production factors external to the organization. Wealth creation is also related to profits and to growth in terms of income, market share, and, above all, the value of the company's shares. This indicator is useful, but quite limited. Actually, the capacity to generate wealth is difficult to measure. Improvements in staff hiring and training practices, good leadership, strong motivation, successful new product research and development strategies and a suitable competitive strategy, to name only a few, will bring an increase in company value over the medium- and long-term that is difficult to quantify in advance.

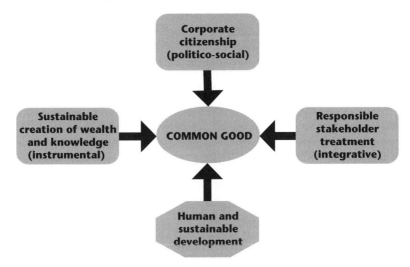

FIGURE 5.2   **How business can contribute to the common good of society**

Business should be efficient at wealth creation in a sustainable manner. This is one primordial responsibility related to the specific contribution of business to the common good. As noted above (see pp. 109–110), profits are instrumental, but they play an important role. Profits – in more general terms wealth creation – permits the company to be able to continue to serve society in the longer term, or even to better serve it, by creating more jobs, producing more useful and more affordable products and creating more wealth.

The greatest enemy of long-term survival and sustained growth is the pursuit of short-term profit at the expense of long-term profitability. Selling off assets, cutting expenditure on staff training or reducing investment in research and development (R & D), for example, will improve immediate results; but in some circumstances it may also jeopardize future results. To be responsible, managers need to balance the short term against the long term.

Business firms not only create wealth, they also generate knowledge, which can be a source of wealth. People within a business firm learn by doing and reflecting on their own activity; they learn from success and failure, from a fusion of knowledge coming from different sources and from the knowledge flowing through the business network, both inside and outside the company. New knowledge is also generated by adapting knowledge to new situations, or innovating to solve problems with imagination and creativity. Apart from this, business firms dedicate resources to generating knowledge; sometimes through powerful R & D departments. Management can play an active role in distributing meaningful knowledge within the organization and enabling people within the organization to share insights and experiences.

Responsibility in generating knowledge is related to maintaining the existence of the business and ensuring that it will be sustainable in the long-term. If the knowledge can be transformed into innovations which make for decreased costs, or something appreciated by the market, then it can generate wealth.

Responsible stakeholder treatment

Responsible treatment of stakeholders involves two types of responsibilities: (1) responsibilities of justice and (2) responsibilities of proactive cooperation.

Responsibilities of justice are the first demand of the common good and include respect for people and the environment, giving what is due to each, that is, their rights. These rights include, among others, human rights, which are due to every person, contractual rights coming from legitimate contracts and promises, honoring one's word in fair circumstances, and telling the truth and acting with transparency. Equity in distribution without favoritism is also a responsibility of justice. Last, but not least, compliance with the law, unless the law is openly contrary to human rights or some other fundamental ethical requirement. Table 5.1 (overleaf) presents some specific duties of justice in the relationship between the firm and its stakeholders.

The *responsibilities of proactive cooperation* go beyond obligations of justice. This requires the responsibility to promote mutual cooperation, even if it is not guaranteed that your concern for others will receive an equivalent return. These responsibilities are rooted in the interdependence between the firm and its stakeholders and the consideration of the humanity inherent in each stakeholder. They are a consequence of intelligent love (see pp. 38–40), and probably a source of mutual benefit.

This cooperation requires, first of all, seeking to avoid *negative impacts* of the activities of the firm toward the stakeholder to a degree that goes beyond a duty of justice. Second, showing a real concern to increase *positive impacts* for the wellbeing and development of stakeholders. Consider, for instance, advertising – a particular relationship with potential buyers. A responsibility of justice is to avoid using misleading or indecent advertising. Proactive cooperative responsibility would be to make the company's advertising contribute to spreading human values (service, friendship, loyalty, honesty and so on), which can foster true human attitudes in all kinds of relationships, including commerce. While the responsibilities of justice are strictly of obligation, generally well-defined and often required by law, responsibilities of proactive cooperation are quite generic and their form depends on concurrent circumstances and foreseeable consequences.

Among the responsibilities of proactive cooperation, can be included, among other illustrative examples (see Table 5.1), actions to support the professional and human development of employees, harmonization of work–family obligations, supplying appropriate communication channels and attention to minority shareholders, serving clients and customers as you would wish to be served, informing and supporting suppliers to improve their satisfaction and capacities, cooperating with the local community in its interdependence with the firm, striving to create an ethical business climate and a culture with a human quality.

Corporate citizenship

The business firm, in its politico-social function, can be considered as a corporate citizen. Obviously, companies do not have individual rights within a nation such as rights to a passport or to vote in elections, but companies participate in society in a similar way to individual citizens by paying taxes, trying to influence governments or supranational organizations (*lobbying*), engaging in free speech, and also expecting infrastructures, legal guarantees and certain protections from the State. In addition, many companies contribute to social needs and cultural and sports events in different ways, including donations, promoting *corporate volunteering* for some social issues and so on. Unlike most individual citizens, an increasing number of companies have not only national but international scope, and act as global corporate citizens.

Companies act as corporate citizens in three ways.[24] One is through the firm's *regular activity*; a second is through *corporate social activities* which seek to tackle some social need, for which a business firm has some particular capacity. A third is *engaging in public policies*, for instance, working for civil rights and freedoms, fostering family values,

TABLE 5.1 **Some examples of corporate responsibilities toward stakeholders**

JUSTICE	PROACTIVE COOPERATION
SHAREHOLDERS AND INVESTORS	
<ul><li>Acting with diligence and loyalty to increase the value of the company's shares.</li><li>Investing with prudence and assuming a prudent level of risk that is appropriate to the company and to shareholder expectations.</li><li>Providing clear, transparent, relevant and honest corporate reports and financial statements.</li><li>Avoiding increasing the company's debt to the extent that bonds and preferred shares are seriously affected, beyond what bond holders and shareholders might reasonably anticipate.</li><li>Treating all shareholders fairly, without discriminating against small investors.</li></ul>	<ul><li>Explaining clearly the company's goals and the means it intends to use to achieve them.</li><li>Providing extensive, honest information on management performance, demonstrating a willingness to respond to shareholders' questions and inquiries and encouraging extensive involvement in the company.</li><li>Taking measures to ensure that the legitimate interests of small shareholders are protected.</li><li>Supervising management appropriately.</li><li>Promoting awareness of the common good and responsibility toward other stakeholders, especially the more vulnerable.</li></ul>
EMPLOYEES	
<ul><li>Avoid treating employees as mere productive instruments or passive receivers of orders.</li><li>Promoting respect for the human rights of workers, including hygiene and safety in the workplace, fair performance assessments, equal opportunities without unjust discrimination, respect for workers' privacy and reputation, workers' right to a fair hearing in cases of disciplinary action or dismissal, etc.</li><li>Complying with fair labor laws on hiring, workers' rights, dismissal, etc. and acting beyond the law if some particular human right is not sufficiently protected.</li></ul>	<ul><li>Favoring an active dialogue with employees and participation in decision-making, even improving their training so that they are capable of greater participation.</li><li>Developing a leadership and an organizational culture which favors human development.</li><li>Fostering initiative, independence, responsibility and creativity at work.</li><li>Providing stable employment as much as possible.</li><li>Giving employees the necessary training to maintain employability.</li><li>Fostering an appropriate work–life balance and adopting family-friendly policies.</li></ul>

JUSTICE	PROACTIVE COOPERATION
EMPLOYEES cont.	
■ Paying workers a just salary that allows them to live decently, in line with the work done, the worker's status, the company's economic situation, and the national economy. ■ Providing the necessary information and training to enable workers to perform their tasks. ■ Allocating positions, tasks, benefits, workloads, awards and penalties according to principles of distributive justice (objective criteria established with practical wisdom). ■ Acting with due diligence in employees' claims and equity in dismissal process.	■ Taking care of employees' personal problems, particularly those that have implications for their work (through assistance programs, personalized attention, etc.)
CUSTOMERS AND CONSUMERS	
■ Fair marketing practices, avoiding all kinds of commercial fraud. ■ Fair contracting practices, including keeping promises on conditions of supply. ■ Giving objective information and labeling products with true, accurate and relevant information. ■ Selling safe and quality products (with no hidden flaws) and telling buyers everything they have a right to know about them. ■ Respecting client privacy and protecting clients' data. ■ Selling at a fair price in relation to product cost and quality and buyers' expectations. ■ Avoiding monopolistic abuses in exploiting buyers' needs. ■ Avoiding deceit in promotions and advertising, and abusive sales methods (violation of privacy, coercion, etc.).	■ Responding quickly to customer complaints, inquiries, suggestions and requests. ■ Encouraging an active dialogue with customers. ■ Developing new products and services in response to customer needs. ■ Promoting sustainable consumption. ■ Favoring education and awareness in consumer issues. ■ Fostering access to essential services for life (adequate food, clothing, shelter, health care, education, public utilities, water and sanitation).

JUSTICE	PROACTIVE COOPERATION
CUSTOMERS AND CONSUMERS cont.	
■ Obtaining contracts without bribes or any other form of corruption. ■ Reporting corrupt trading practices to the authorities.	
SUPPLIERS	
■ Complying with contracts and commitments, and honoring offers that have been accepted. ■ Using fair procedures for awarding contracts. ■ Avoiding complicity in unfair practices in the supply chain. ■ Not abusing a position of power relations when there are changes, e.g., when a supplier is in difficulties. ■ Not using ideas or suggestions provided by suppliers without notification or permission, or without agreeing compensation.	■ Providing opportunities for suppliers to make a fair profit. ■ Keeping suppliers informed of developments inside the company and projects that may affect them in the future. ■ Providing information or technical assistance to loyal suppliers to maintain technology or quality requirements. ■ Building a stable relationship or a degree of exclusivity with loyal suppliers that contributes to their long-term survival, without taking advantage of the firm's dominant position.
LOCAL COMMUNITY	
■ Respecting local regulations, standards and customs unless they are ethically unacceptable. ■ Avoiding damaging the local community or environment (abuse of natural resources, pollution, waste). ■ Minimizing damage caused to the local community and/or environment and providing adequate compensation, if negative external effects are unavoidable. ■ Using advertising that respects local people and the community's cultural values.	■ Fostering employment and wealth creation for the local community. ■ Contributing to improving the physical, social and cultural local environment. ■ Supporting cultural events of the local community which can foster human development. ■ Investing in the community. ■ Fostering corporate volunteering in the community.
COMPETITORS	
■ Not telling lies about competitors' products or services.	■ Avoiding comparative advertising.

JUSTICE	PROACTIVE COOPERATION
COMPETITORS cont.	
▪ Avoiding advertising that contains personal attacks on competitors or that makes false or misleading comparisons. ▪ Not selling at "cut-throat" prices to strangle the competition. ▪ Avoiding agreements with competitors for price collusion or division of markets and avoiding any other form of unfair competition, including monopolistic practices that undermine legitimate competition.	▪ Seeking agreements with competitors that benefit the common good (e.g., promoting fair laws and/or ethical codes for the whole industry, agreement to promote economic development).

fighting against discrimination, contributing to political campaigns and lobbying. The latter may be problematic if abuses occur and there is infringement of democracy and equality given the power and resources of large companies. We will focus on the firm's regular activity and on corporate social activities.

In its *regular activity*, the firm indirectly contributes to society through two responsibilities already mentioned. Sustainable wealth and knowledge creation, although directly for the benefit of the firm, are indirectly contributions to the whole of society. On making profits, businesses pay taxes and a great part of the knowledge generated in a firm will sooner or later spread out into society. Acting with a sense of sustainability, business, first of all, avoids negative impacts on people and on the environment. Similarly, treating stakeholders responsibly is also a relevant contribution to society.

Apart from these indirect contributions, business firms in their regular activity favor the wellbeing of society in two important matters. One is *maintaining and creating jobs*. A responsible company will do everything in its power to maintain employees and, if it can, create new jobs. In most cases, this will be achieved through reasonable growth or by entering into new businesses, while at the same time developing the necessary skills among the workforce and improving their working conditions. However, this responsibility must be harmonized with maintaining the competitiveness of the business. This means not maintaining unnecessary jobs that put the company at a permanent competitive disadvantage and can ultimately jeopardize the whole firm.

Another important contribution of the firm to society is the development, production or distribution of *products and services*, often with an important degree of innovation. In this way, business makes products available for society which can be a support for human development and at prices which, by combining efficient production systems and free market competition, make them more accessible to the population.

In addition, business makes a significant contribution to the common good by respectful corporate behavior towards the *environment*, and encouraging consumers to responsible and sustainable behavior, too.

Companies respect and care for the environment by (1) making efficient and sustainable use of resources, (2) avoiding pollution, (3) preventing waste, recycling and disposing of waste, packaging and obsolete products, (4) contributing to the mitigation of and adaptation to climate change and (5) protecting the natural environment and biodiversity, and restoring natural habitats.

Striving for the *continuity and sustainability* of the firm is also such a basic responsibility that other responsibilities would not be met if this is not done effectively; this permits the firm's existence and competitive ability over time.

Corporate social activities are different in that they are not directly related to the company's core activity, but they are a contribution of the business firm to the common good in some aspect in which it has certain ability. Hiring disabled people, integrating immigrant workers and other marginalized groups, supporting universities and research centers and extending professional training are just a few of the social issues in which companies can collaborate to solve society's problems. Companies can also share their accumulated experience or assign some of their managers or employees to provide advice or management expertise on social issues in which they have a special competence (new technologies, organizational methods, etc.). Apart from these, companies may possess the means to improve the socio-cultural environment (e.g., by distributing cultural products or supporting social activities, or even by exerting pressure to have certain laws or customs changed). In addition, companies can provide economic resources to sponsor artistic, cultural and sporting events, or make donations to charity.

Some see corporate social activities, inappropriately considered by some as the exclusive corporate social responsibility, as a matter of public relations or even as a danger. Michael E. Porter and Mark R. Kramer[25] have a different view. While they criticize arbitrary choices of social activities of companies, they argue that social responsibility is a *business opportunity* if companies determine carefully their social activities by identifying the social consequences of their actions and discovering opportunities to benefit society and themselves by strengthening the competitive context in which they operate.

This is not an ethical argument, but a pragmatic justification. However, such initiatives are welcomed under this win-win strategy. The question is whether there are any ethical reasons for a company to undertake social activities and whether or not these can bring about competitive advantages. Do companies have moral legitimacy to contribute to solving social problems or are social problems the exclusive responsibility of the State?

The answer is that social problems, first of all, belong to society rather than to the State, so it is society itself that must address them first. According to the socio-ethical principle of subsidiarity (see p. 96) – in short, giving support to lesser organizations without absorbing them – the State must intervene wherever social initiative and solidarity are insufficient, or if it seems that the problem will not be solved without the intervention of the State. *State intervention* – which obviously has to be paid for by *civil society* and thus entails heavier taxes and more bureaucracy – is detrimental to *freedom of initiative* and lacks the human warmth and effectiveness of direct action by those closest to the problem.

Obviously, companies are not charitable institutions, but that does not mean they can blithely ignore what is going on in society. *Companies are part of society*; therefore, they should not overlook their immediate responsibilities, but contribute, along with other social institutions and individuals, to improving their social environment to the best of their ability.

To sum up, it does not seem that social activities can be systematically ignored by business, large and small companies alike. However, given the circumstances, there are many needs that companies will not be able to attend to, or will only be able to give limited attention. It would not be right for a company to attend to social activities if doing so meant neglecting basic duties of justice. Nevertheless, corporate concern for social problems, apart from being very valuable in itself, can become a source of competitive advantage.

MANAGING HUMAN AND SUSTAINABLE BUSINESS

There is a *business logic* understood in pure economic terms, which has been mainstream for years, where ethics has been seen as a mere tool for economic results. In contrast there is a *holistic logic* of business where economic, human, social and environmental dimensions are considered together. Managing human and sustainable business takes this latter perspective.

In managing sustainable business, economic prosperity should be sound, but at the same time positive impacts on people and society, and the environment are also promoted. Concern for *people and society* includes employees' needs and rights, including health, safety and opportunities for training and development within the company, participation of employees in business activities and the fostering of an entrepreneurial culture. It also includes community involvement of a business and any business activity in favour of its social environment. *Concern for the environment* focuses on the use of raw materials, renewable and non-renewable resources, ecologically destructive practices, conservation and the use of energy, pollution in all its forms caused by business activity, waste produced and its eventual disposal, along with other issues related to environmental sustainability.

Striving to meet economic, environmental and social demands is commonly termed managing toward the *Triple Bottom Line*. The three aspects are not seen as three different levels on which to make decisions, but as a whole. That means it is not a number of human-social and environmental issues added to conventional business but a harmonious integration of these dimensions. It requires permanent commitment from management and everyone within the business firm, and effective integration of sustainability into all processes, products and manufacturing activities. Holistic decision-making, as mentioned before (see pp. 50–52), is consistent with managing a sustainable business.

Solving conflicts between two or more of the sustainable dimensions requires practical wisdom (see pp. 40–42) to find the *golden mean* in the fulfillment of all responsibilities. In the long run, many conflicts eventually disappear of their own accord. Respect for human rights and human development of workers may lead to poorer economic results in the short term, but more highly motivated, more cooperative, better trained and more ethically aware employees, who will probably make the results improve in the not-too-distant future.

Selecting some priorities should be an effective way to change a firm into a sustainable business. The norm ISO 26000 – *Guidance on Social Responsibility* proposes a reasonable and useful guide to these priorities by considering business influence on society and the environment, focusing on some key elements. These include the identification of characteristic and general impacts of the organization, stakeholders who receive business impacts, their interests and expectations along with those of society, the evaluation of the sphere of business influence and how this influence is exercised, acting with due diligence. Then, the relevance and priority of matters and actions to undertake should be defined.

As basic elements of a responsible organizational policy which leads to sustainability, this document suggests seven principles: (1) *accountability*, which means that management is answerable to the supervisory authorities of an organization, to legal authorities and to society in general; (2) *transparency*, which means that organizations should disclose their policies and activities and their likely impact on society in an accurate and readily available manner; (3) *ethical behavior*, which should be the standard of corporate behavior, including honesty, equity and integrity; (4) *respect for stakeholder interests,* including the rights and legitimate interests of all groups that affect or can be affected by corporate policy; (5) *respect for the rule of law*, which constitutes a mandatory corporate obligation to obey national and international law; (6) *respect for international norms of behavior*, which mainly refers to international standards concerning environmental protection, workers' rights or fighting corruption, especially in those countries where such rights are not protected or enforced by governmental institutions; and (7) *respect for human rights*, which is seen as a universal principle of corporate behavior and is not negotiable.

These principles are the result of a certain international consensus, rather than a systematic ethics-based approach as is presented here, but give an idea of the current sensibility in matters of current concern relating to responsibility and sustainability.

EXECUTIVE SUMMARY

Managing business involves a tension between making profits and being responsible. Historically, several arguments have been given for favoring corporate responsibility: responsibility harmonized with profits; responsibility associated with power; responsibility that avoided risk and promoted reputation. Currently there are pressures for such behavior from primary stakeholders of the firm, from governments and institutions and from the social environment. All of these pressures are more or less related to the bottom line, and so responsibility can be seen as a necessity for profits. However, there are also moral motives which provide arguments for managing business with responsibility and sustainability.

Profits permit the maintaining of the firm with its services to society; they make a fair return on investment possible and fleeing to other businesses less likely, and they also stimulate new investment and the creation of jobs. Without profits a business firm cannot survive in the long term. But making profits is not the only purpose of business in society. Business is justified in its contribution to the common good of society through its specific activity of providing goods and services with profit. Other contributions to the common good are associated with this goal. In line with this, the purpose of business in society is presented through a common good stakeholder approach, which goes beyond the conventional shareholder and stakeholder approaches.

The responsibilities of business in society can be considered by seeing the firm as being three types of functions with their respective contributions to the common good and their corresponding responsibilities to make such contributions: responsibility in creating wealth and knowledge efficiently (instrumental function), in responsible stakeholder treatment (integrative function) and in being a good corporate citizen (politico-social function). Responsible stakeholder treatment involves responsibilities of justice and responsibilities of cooperation. Corporate citizenship entails contributions to the common good through the company's core activities and social activities as corporate contributions oriented to solving social problems. Engaging in public policies is also part of corporate citizenship, but this should be carefully analyzed in each situation to avoid infringements of democracy and equality, given the power and resources of large companies.

Managing human and sustainable business entails taking into account how business influences human development and focusing on sustainability through a holistic view of its economic, social and environmental dimensions. This means seeking not only economic results, but also positive impacts on society and the environment. Sustainability should be integrated into all processes, products and manufacturing activities and every decision should be considered with practical wisdom.

CHAPTER 6

MORAL COMPETENCIES OF
THE MANAGER

The endurance of organization depends upon the quality of leadership; and that quality derives from the breadth of the morality upon which it rests.[1]

CHESTER I. BARNARD (1886–1961)
Pioneer in management theory

Chester Irving Barnard, an American business executive and pioneer in management theory, was one of the first in pointing out the importance of leadership in organizations. He put special emphasis on cooperation and on the responsibility of the executive to promote this. In his influential book *The Functions of the Executive*, published in 1938, he wrote: "Close study of the structure of organization or of its dynamic processes may induce an overemphasis upon some one or several of the more technical aspects of cooperation."[2] Facing such overemphasis, he saw leadership "as the factor of chief significance in human cooperation".[3] He made clear that the moral factor is very important in creating trust – "faith" in Barnard's words – but he also stressed that this factor alone is not sufficient to achieve cooperation. Structure and process are also important.

Barnard's words emphasize that two elements are essential in management: the technical, related to structures and processes, and the ethical, related to trust and leadership. The former requires skills, the latter virtues. Barnard here as elsewhere offered a deep vision of reality. However, his suggestion, to a great extent, was ignored and, for years, many emphasized only the technical side and consequently, the importance of managerial skills.

The situation started to change when in 1977 Abraham Zaleznik of the Harvard Business School criticized the incompleteness of an exclusively technical vision of management, arguing that it lost sight of inspiration, vision and the full spectrum of human drives and desires.[4] He postulated that managers – skilled in technique – and leaders are two very different types of people, and business needs both managers, with technical training, and leaders, with capacity to generate trust. Nowadays, it is generally accepted that these two types should converge in the profile of the business executive. Both technical and strategic skills and leadership qualities are necessary. The latter has to do with trust and credibility, and ultimately with ethics and virtues, which are at the core of moral competencies as we will see in this chapter. Managers should lead people within the organization, motivating them and promoting a sense of collaboration and cooperation toward common goals. In other words, managers, especially in acting as leaders, need a variety of competencies. We will begin with an overview of competencies in managing and leading business firms. Then we will focus on moral competencies.

PERSONAL COMPETENCIES IN BUSINESS FIRMS

The idea of personal competencies, or simply "competencies", has increasingly been used in selecting, developing and supporting managers in business firms. Although there are several definitions, it is generally understood that competencies are personal abilities for excellence in performance of a certain task or profession; or, in more general terms, as has been said: "Competencies represent who an individual is and what an individual knows and does."[5]

The concept of competencies was introduced in the selection of personnel in the 1970s as an alternative to intelligence tests, the relevance of which was being questioned. Instead, an analysis of some behavioral indicators determined for successful performance of the job was proposed. Thus, the concept of competencies emerged. Their determination and identification are generally conducted by an expert through interviewing and observing performance.[6] More recently, it has been suggested that the development of organizations that use competency approaches promises to raise a number of new opportunities, and ultimately effectiveness.[7]

In practice, many lists of managerial competencies have been offered,[8] and different scholars propose schemes to classify or group competencies, by considering a variety of criteria. One possible way to group them is through four categories. The first three directly address performance, and can be termed technique-oriented, goal-oriented and relation-oriented. The fourth relates to moral character; and while not directly addressed at performance, it may have a substantial influence on the others.

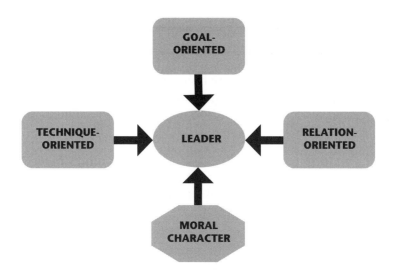

FIGURE 6.1 **Types of leader's competencies**

■ *Technique-oriented competencies* refer to capacities for effectiveness in working. Mentioned among these[9] are capacities related to analyzing data; planning and organizing, applying specialist technical capability and technology, developing job knowledge and expertise and sharing knowledge with others; meeting customer expectations; adapting and responding to change, being open to new ideas, dealing effectively with ambiguity and coping with pressure and setbacks; working productively in a stressful environment (resilience); openness to experience, confidence, credibility, risk tolerance and tenacity; and also competencies related to technical learning and research.

■ *Goal-oriented competencies* are related to discovering opportunities and providing a sharp vision for the future; creating and innovating, contributing with new ideas and insights, creating innovative products and solutions, and seeking opportunities for organizational change and improvement; formulating strategies and concepts and working strategically to attain organizational goals, and taking into account a wide range of issues that impact on the organization; deciding on and initiating action, and making effective decisions, even in difficult circumstances; setting clear objectives, planning activities well in advance; taking initiative and assuming responsibility, focusing on customer needs and satisfaction, setting high standards for quality and quantity, and consistently achieving set goals.

■ *Relation-oriented competencies* include working with people, promoting cooperation, building team spirit and motivating people;

persuading and influencing others; leading, supervising and coaching people; relating, networking and negotiating; delegating and empowering individuals, managing conflict and communicating efficiently. The latter includes writing and reporting and speaking clearly and fluently, expressing opinions and arguments clearly and convincingly, and making presentations with confidence.

■ *Moral competencies.* Some authors mention competencies such as acting with consideration, concern and care for individuals; adhering to principles and values; behaving with justice and integrity and promoting ethical values, demonstrating commitment to the organization, self-awareness, conscientiousness; and courage. These are moral competencies rooted in the moral character, as we will discuss in the following section. They have a direct influence in leadership through other competencies, especially those that are relation-oriented.

THE MANAGER'S MORAL CHARACTER AS A SOURCE OF COMPETENCIES

Moral competencies, and more specifically character and virtues, have a particular importance in leadership, and on how leadership is exercised. Character shapes the vision, goals, strategies, perceptions and other key dimensions of the leader.[10] For a long time, leadership was attributed to charisma, but as shown by Y. Sankar the quest for leadership excellence is based more on character than charisma.[11]

The relevance of moral character in leadership has been highlighted by several outstanding authors. "It is character through which leadership is exercised", said Peter F. Drucker.[12] Henry Mintzberg agreed that character is the most important competence for the leader's effectiveness, along with the individual's insight, vision and intuition.[13] The moral character of the leader and their concerns for self and others is also stressed in *Authentic Transformational Leadership*, which has become one of the mainstream leadership theories.[14]

In the age of globalization, Judi Brownell, a respected author on people management, has pointed out: "it is essential for global leaders to be men and women of integrity and character", adding that "personal qualities required to create and maintain trust and to generate goodwill distinguish the truly effective global leader".[15]

Joanne B. Ciulla, a recognized expert in leadership, showed that ethics is at the core of leadership,[16] while Alejo J. Sison, drawing from several case studies and further arguments, affirmed that virtues are the leader's moral capital,[17] and Alan Kolp and Peter Rea suggested that leadership is a character-based matter.[18]

To conclude this small sample, we might mention Kenneth Andrews, former professor of Harvard Business School, who was convinced that "inquiring into character should therefore be part of all executive selection – as well as all executive development within the corporation".[19]

As noted in Chapter 1 (see pp. 11–12), character is shaped by virtues, which are good habits acquired with effort through conscious and free good acts. Virtues are understood as stable dispositions of the human individual which provide inner strength for acting well. Vices act in a similar way but in the opposite sense. Thus, a courageous individual tends to act courageously, and a ruthless person has a tendency to act ruthlessly. Virtues are, therefore, much more than simple temperamental dispositions, but are routines acquired with a certain automatism, and included in one's personality.

Moral competencies in leadership are nothing other than virtues which provide an example and promote the trust and willingness of people to follow the leader. Theoretical and empirical research suggest that people are influenced by observing role models and learn about appropriate behavior vicariously through witnessing what is rewarded and what is punished, or which actions attract attention and which do not.[20] Managers can foster good or bad behavior through their interpersonal relationships with their subordinates and their behaviors.[21]

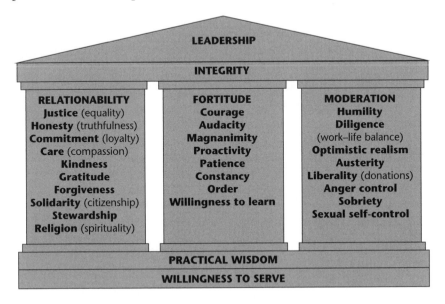

FIGURE 6.2 **Moral competencies which make up leadership**

There are two stable dispositions of character which can be found at the core of other virtues; namely willingness to serve and practical wisdom. The former, related to intelligent love and benevolence (see pp. 38–40) is embedded in all other virtues. Practical wisdom helps one determine the "golden mean" of virtues.

Other moral competencies, which are real pillars of leadership, regulate three basic human tendencies: (1) the *relational tendency* of the human being, balancing both the inclinations to keep for oneself and to share with others what one possesses, (2) the *tendency to strive* to obtain whatever is seen as valuable, avoiding both cowardice and temerity and (3) the *tendency to enjoy* emotions and desires for what one finds pleasant, avoiding any excess. A number of virtues which regulate these tendencies can be grouped as competencies related with *relationability*, *fortitude* and *moderation* respectively. Finally, there is a stable disposition of character which expresses a harmonious unity to all virtues: *integrity* (see Figure 6.2).

WILLINGNESS TO SERVE, A KEY COMPETENCY FOR LEADERSHIP

Probably the primary feature of an authentic leader is his or her willingness to serve others with a sense of selflessness, and even self-sacrifice. This requires concern for other people, helping them to achieve worthy objectives. The opposite of serving others is using people for one's own interests, but this is an expression of power. When a supposed leader only has power then potential *followers* will follow the *leader* to obtain some reward, but not as a consequence of a deeper motivation beyond this. This is *transactional leadership*, where the links between the leader and the follower fully depend on the incentives offered as rewards. They are weak and expensive.

A different option is presented by the *transformational leadership* theory, which proposes increasing motivation in followers through a positive change in their values, attitudes and willingness to cooperate. This goal requires a leader with the personality, traits and ability to make the change. *Authentic transformational leaders* are seen as moral exemplars of working toward the benefit of the team or community. In addition, an individualized consideration of the followers is presented in the later versions of this theory. This includes listening to the follower's concerns and needs, giving them empathy and support, keeping communication open and placing challenges before them. This leadership fosters aspirations for self-development in followers and intrinsic motivation for their tasks.[22] All of these can be included in a framework of willingness to serve.

Willingness to serve is even more essential in the theory of *Servant Leadership*,[23] which defines leaders as those who want to serve others and, thus, foster a similar attitude in their followers. Authors in line with this theory[24] mention, among other qualities of a leader, the ability to withdraw and reorient oneself in the direction of self-improvement, acceptance and empathy toward others, listening to them and seeking to understand them, as well as foresight, awareness, perception, persuasion, healing and serving. Concern for others' needs and willingness to serve are also central in the Juan A. Pérez-López[25] approach, which emphasizes the connection of willingness to serve with practical rationality and virtues. This author suggests two types of manager's behaviors to develop the motivation to serve others. First, do not prevent one's subordinates from acting in accordance with this kind of motivation. Second, teach them to evaluate the consequences their actions will have on others, asking in what way one's own action can contribute to satisfying others' needs.[26]

Willingness to serve is neither sentimentalism nor an indulgent attitude toward people's desires, but concern for their authentic human needs through intelligent love (see pp. 38–40). Following others' desires blindly rather than exercising good leadership would be an irresponsible way of running an organization.

Developing willingness to serve requires being sensitive to the *authentic needs* and *legitimate expectations* of those around one, including needs linked to their wellbeing and professional and human development. However, authentic service should avoid a lack of respect for the person's privacy and autonomy. This means maintaining a distance from intrusiveness into personal life and paternalism.

When a person serves others unselfishly, he or she is developing one of the highest human capacities and thus flourishing as a human being. Within an organization, serving others can awaken a desire to serve in those who are served. A sincere and persistent attitude of concern for others usually develops trust and willingness to help, while selfishness leads to the opposite.

PRACTICAL WISDOM

It would be worth remembering here that practical wisdom helps one to determine how virtue is to be expressed in each concrete situation when two extreme opposites are available, one which is characterized by its excess and the other by its deficiencies (see pp. 40–42). In the words of Aristotle, "virtue makes the goal right, practical wisdom the things leading to it".[27] So to act with justice (virtue) we need to know what is "just" (indicated by practical wisdom); and we can see the same pattern with the other virtues. Practical wisdom helps one to determine with sensibility what it is to be generous, moderate or courageous in each situation. With absolute correctness the Ancients called prudence "the helmsman of the other virtues" (*auriga virtutum*).

Good judgment

Practical wisdom is the virtue of good judgment. It leads to *deliberation* about events from the ethical perspective, analyzing, considering or seeking advice. It is also shown in the *choice* of an ethically correct alternative and acting with *drive* when putting the decisions taken into practice: what has been clearly identified as being good to do must not be left as a mere decision, it has to be implemented with determination within the appropriate time and without undue delay.

A lack of practical wisdom, in terms of good judgment, is shown in different ways. One is *superficiality* in analyzing problems; the failure to check with someone who could offer a prudent and expert viewpoint; *too hasty* decisions; *inconsistency* in reasoning; *negligence* or carelessness in seeking relevant information or in being aware of moral aspects. Negligence often results in error and omission in the very responsibilities of the office, or when a manager is concentrated on technical, economic or political aspects and neglects concern for people. *Cunning*, that is the ability to find deceitful or illicit means to achieve the given objective, is also contrary to prudence. Prudence, in contrast to cunning, helps one discover what is good, to distinguish the licit means from the illicit to achieve good objectives.

The manager with practical wisdom has good criteria to act well in each situation. The importance of prudence for the tasks of management and governance is reflected in some words attributed to the emperor Marcus Aurelius, on the occasion of his coronation. His prayer to the gods took the form: "Grant me the strength to change what I can change, the resignation to accept what I can't change, and above all, the discernment to be able to tell one from the other."

Responsibility

Responsibility is also related to practical wisdom. It refers to being aware of the self-determination of one's own actions and consequently being answerable or accountable for one's own decisions and actions and their predictable consequences, including the effects on those who are affected by the action (stakeholders). Conducting oneself responsibly is a positive character trait, a sign of maturity and a competency which fosters trustworthiness.

Being responsible entails taking decisions with weighed deliberation, seeking sincerely sound moral reasons to justify them (*antecedent responsibility*) and assuming their predictable consequences (*consequent responsibility*). Inasmuch as particular decisions are not isolated from life as a whole, responsibility entails acting in harmony with what one is (or would like to be), an honorable person, a religious individual, a committed person with social concern and so on. Thus, being responsible is also acting with consistency, and making decisions by contemplating one's vision of life and applying the values which one sincerely considers are the right ones (*congruent responsibility*). This latter responsibility can be closely related to a sense of professional vocation or other personal calling to carry out a certain mission in the world (*transcendent responsibility*), and might be strong in some professionals such as doctors, nurses or teachers, but, in a certain sense, it can be found in any noble human work. Managing business can also be considered as a calling,[28] and managers considered to be endowed with a sense of professional responsibility.

Responsibility in its four forms[29] is expressed as a stable disposition to careful deliberation on the goodness of an action and its consequences, and awareness of the congruence between a decision and one's life and the requirements which one's professional vocation involve.

MORAL COMPETENCIES RELATED TO RELATIONABILITY

The human being has a tendency to keep to oneself but also to share with others what one possesses (thoughts, feelings and material possessions). Moral competencies of relationability regulate these tendencies, strengthening character to avoid acting with *egoism*, that is, with self-interest disrespectful to other people's rights, and helping one to act with respect, care and intelligent love toward others. It also pushes us to share in a reasonable way.

Justice and equity

An elemental willingness to serve is to be just and act with fairness. As noted (see pp. 33–36), justice refers to that due of an individual or a group to another, or to society as a whole, or to another member of society on account of his or her merits or necessities (see pp. 33–36). As a virtue, justice is normally defined as the perpetual and constant will to render to each his or her right. Thus, a manager is just when he or she has the stable disposition to respect the rights of others in both intention and in action, not sometimes but continuously. He or she also acts with fairness in carrying out distribution with *equity*, without bias, when the task is required.

Justice is the minimum ethical requirement in dealing with people and must never be suppressed. Apart from the moral obligation, employees are generally very sensitive in matters related to justice, and it is difficult to imagine that a manager can become a leader if he or she commits injustice.

Honesty and truthfulness

Honesty means "telling the truth, being told what you are getting, or at least, what you are letting yourself in for".[30] There is no doubt that honesty is one of the touchstones of professionalism and of corporate responsibility, and even "the first virtue of business life".[31] An honest manager generates credibility and trust. In contrast, an environment where deception and lies are permitted becomes increasingly strained and will eventually be terrible both for people and for its governance. Telling the truth no matter what is appreciated and generates admiration. A manager who is truthful, clear, frank and sincere in communication attracts, while the opposing attitudes such as duplicity, dissimulation and hypocrisy tend to provoke rejection.

Truthfulness is central in honesty, in the sense defined above, but truthfulness is more than this. Truthfulness is love for the truth, and is shown through a permanent attitude to search for the truth and to act in accordance with one's own thoughts in one's words and deeds.

One especially pertinent aspect of truthfulness is acting with *transparency* by providing the relevant information to which each (person or group) has a right. To this end, the manager has to begin with a consideration of what information has to be given to each *stakeholder*: the shareholders (the truth about the use of their capital and reasonable expectations that they can harbor); the workers (the truth about the situation of the company in relation to their work); the clients and customers (substantial information about the product, safety or security measures required to use the product, guarantee of availability of replacements, etc.); the suppliers (truth about solvency to pay for the supplies); and the general public (avoiding misleading or biased information to discredit the competition, etc.).

Commitment and virtuous loyalty

In some contexts a certain "disconnected culture" in which people avoid strong and permanent commitments is quite common. However, being committed to pledge or obligate one's own self to noble causes usually brings about admiration and trust when such commitment is honored with loyalty. Of course, there are ignoble commitments and loyalties, the Mafia being a well-known example. But this is *pseudo-loyalty*, not *virtuous loyalty*.

Broadly speaking, loyalty can be seen as a mere utilitarian adherence to a product, branch, company, for example, as in the case of "customer loyalty"; this, however, is not a virtue. An emotional sense of belonging or giving support, maybe to a sports club or the company for which one works, also stops short of being an expression of virtue. Loyalty as a virtue is a willingness to commit oneself to a good cause and persevere over time with such a commitment. Loyalty is also honoring one's own word, but only, of course, if the word is given with regard to something good.

As with any other virtue, loyalty is regulated by practical wisdom. Loyalty is far from an irrational or blind enthusiasm, which is disconnected, or a mercenary approach in which money is the only concern binding one to work. Being a part of a community such as a business firm requires a commitment to work loyally for its legitimate interests. This can be extended to teams or groups of people committed to working for common goals.

Breaking serious and legitimate commitments freely undertaken openly runs against loyalty and such action strongly erodes the leadership of those who commit the betrayal. In contrast, loyal leaders contribute to heightened cohesion and cooperation within the firm.

Care and compassion

As noted (see pp. 38–39 and 84–86), care focuses on understanding relationships as a response to another person, and paying attention to his or her needs. Care is related to *compassion*, meaning feeling pity for other people's needs. Compassion gives one the capacity to be aware of others' distress together with a desire to relieve it.

Compassionate managers can deal with "toxic emotions", including indignation, frustration and dissatisfaction in corporate life.[32] Some empirical research based on narratives identified manners in which compassion is demonstrated and facilitated in organizations, and its effects on human and organizational behaviors.[33]

Understanding people's failures is also an important aspect of compassion, but compassion is not sentimentalism. Thus, compassion, along with a sense of justice, prevents passivity or looking the other way when one is aware of some wrongdoing on the part of a collaborator or subordinate. He or she should be warned or corrected whenever necessary with tact, in positive terms and by providing guidance and support.

Kindness

Kindness refers to showing sympathy or understanding; being humane, considerate and adopting a friendly, generous and warm-hearted attitude. It is neither a severe manner nor excessively mild or soft behavior. These are not external forms or simply good manners in dealing with people. Far from conventionalism, pleasant manners of virtuous kindness are an expression of humility, respect and the desire to serve others.

Kindness, in a sense, includes virtues such as *meekness, gentleness, affability* and *good manners*, being approachable, easy and pleasant to speak to. Kindness can also include a moderate and opportune sense of humor and fun.

Delicacy in relations is highly suitable for the manager and for leadership. It is opposed to sterile violence, to the fruitless spending of forces, and to anger which is senseless and often born out of something trifling. When delicacy is absent, bad-tempered rows and disproportionate anger often appear, which weaken the most solid of arguments, cause bitterness and feuds, diminish energy for work, heighten the irascibility of those offended, and have them mulling over the perceived insult and plotting revenge. The lack of delicacy in relations in the company erodes cordiality and the trust which, in some way, leads to good results.

Gratitude

Gratitude leads one to be appreciative of benefits received. It is not only a matter of feeling it but also of showing it in an appropriate way. Although gratitude can be expressed in words, it is above all an inner attitude of appreciation for those who have favored us. Gratitude is not reciprocity, which requires giving something equivalent without the sincere recognition and appreciation of the other's generosity. This is not to say, though, that gratitude cannot be shown with a gift or present.

Gratitude is a significant virtue in leadership and in organizational life. Although not frequently mentioned among the traits of a leader, common experience shows that people appreciate attitudes of recognition and gratitude when these are due, and look unfavorably on their omission.

Forgiveness

This virtue is characterized by forgiving those who have done wrong, accepting the shortcomings of others, giving people a second chance and not being vengeful. "Forgiveness represents a suite of prosocial changes that occur within an individual who has been offended or damaged by a relationship partner."[34]

Forgiveness is appropriate in situations where feelings of resentment, indignation or anger appear. These feelings can be due to a perceived offence, humiliation or mistakes of others that make one's work more difficult. These feelings can lead to attitudes of non-collaboration, avoidance and even vengeance.

If a leader has these feelings, he or she can become distant from the followers. In contrast, those who are able to forgive are in a good position to find effective reconciliation. Thus, it makes sense to stress the important role that forgiveness has in the leadership of effective organizations.[35]

Solidarity and citizenship

Solidarity is a concept employed in social science, mainly in sociology, to refer to ties in a society or community that bind people to one another. Consequently, solidarity is a description of how societies and communities find cohesion and achieve common goals. Sometimes, solidarity expresses feelings of support and a willingness to help, especially in situations of catastrophe or when people are suffering serious want. Solidarity denotes a union of interest, purpose and concern among members of a group. This is consistent with the etymological meaning of solidarity, taken from the French *solidarité* which signifies "mutual responsibility". This is a word related to *solidaire*, meaning *interdependent, complete, entire*.[36]

Solidarity as a moral competency is related to the existence of interdependences among people within a group sharing common goals. The achievement of these demands mutual responsibility, that is, solidarity. Willingness to serve leads one to discover interdependences and how to treat interdependent people or groups to achieve the common good.

Solidarity as a virtue (moral competency) has been defined as "a firm and persevering determination to commit oneself to the common good". The common good can refer to a particular community, including the business firm with its stakeholders, a nation or even global society.

In corporate life, a manager or an employee with solidarity is a person who shows an effective contribution to the common good of the firm or to a group within the firm, even to the extent of sacrificing personal interests for the interest of the whole. Solidarity leads one to act for whatever will be beneficial for the development of the business firm and can contribute to the flourishing of those involved in it.

Solidarity is close to the notion of *citizenship behavior*, understood not only as a feeling of belonging or identification with a team, group or community, but with a "sense of obligation to the common good that includes the self but that stretches beyond one's self-interest".[38]

Stewardship

The previous virtues regard relationability between humans, but relationability also refers to humans and the *natural environment*. It is not virtuous to either hold a despotic dominion over nature nor to dilute humans into the ecological system as just one more species, without considering the human condition, rational and free, and human dignity (see pp. 30–31). What may be recognizable as virtuous behavior is an attitude of stewardship toward the environment. Stewardship is a careful and responsible management of something entrusted to one's care. In this context, it refers to stewardship of natural resources.

The idea of stewardship has a religious connotation shared in a great degree by the three major monotheistic religions – Judaism, Christianity and Islam. God has entrusted creation to the human being and this has to respect the integrity of the creation. However, secular visions often believe that stewardship of the environment is everyone's responsibility.

Religion and spirituality

Religion is relationability with God or with divinity or, in a broader sense, with someone who is completely outside and beyond the world and gives ultimate meaning to the world and human life. This is what transcendence originally means. For some people, transcendence is reinforced by sacred books or by the belief of a divine revelation. For others, a sense of transcendence comes from believing in a power operating in the universe that is greater than oneself; or even in a sense of interconnectedness with all living creatures. Believing in transcendence, in one way or another, generates *spirituality*, which is a source of meaning and inspiration.

The concept of religion may derive from *religare* (to bind) meaning a bond uniting humans to God. It is essentially a consequence of one's recognition of divine majesty and of our absolute dependence on God. Religion can be found as a stable disposition of character. This is a virtue whose purpose is to render God the worship due to Him as the source of all beings and the principle of all government of things. Religion and spirituality provide a *meaning of life* with important consequences for how the world is understood, and also as a source of values and motivations.

MORAL COMPETENCIES RELATED TO FORTITUDE

There is a human tendency to strive and even fight to obtain whatever is seen as valuable. This tendency can become a disproportionate aggressiveness or, on the contrary, an excessive passivity and lack of effort to *achieve valuable goals* or *resist adversities*. Moral competencies to act with the golden mean in this can be grouped as *fortitude*. Courage, audacity, magnanimity and proactivity refer to fortitude in achieving valuable goals. Other virtues, such as patience, constancy, order and a willingness to learn express strength of character in facing or resisting the adversities.

Courage

Courage pushes one to perform actions which are arduous but worthwhile. Courage is shown in the willpower to carry out a beneficial action in spite of the impediments and obstacles which appear. It moderates the impetus to take more of a risk than would be prudent, and at the same time gives a push that counteracts the spontaneous tendency to withdraw when faced with an outcome that is difficult to reach. It is located, then, at the just mean between temerity and cowardice. The manager may be afraid in the face of the difficulties or uncertainties that appear, and so needs courage. A manager with courage does not search out danger like a reckless adventurer, but will not flee from it like a coward, either. In contrast, courage leads the manager to fight for that which is seen as valuable, using opportune means, and guided by practical wisdom.

Audacity

Audacity leads one to take on risky but feasible tasks which many people would not dare to attempt. It is in opposition to the spinelessness of exaggerating the difficulties unreasonably, until inaction is reached. Audacity is not rash, either, it is simply the brave decision to seek a valuable objective following a calm consideration of the opportunities and the threats. Audacity demands, then, reflection and discernment together with the resolution to say what ought to be said with no silencing of the truth for fear, and to act in a timely fashion, despite the risks involved. Without audacity many entrepreneurs and managers would not have set up their companies, nor achieved any success worthy of praise.

Magnanimity

Magnanimity is the disposition of the spirit toward great things (from the Latin *magnus*, meaning great). Magnanimity pushes one to set great and noble challenges and to involve oneself in achieving them without flinching from the difficulties entailed. Magnanimity involves a *spirit of enterprise* to undertake initiatives that may benefit people, or indeed the whole of society.

Magnanimity should not be confused with a vain love of grandeur, or with visionary proposals that fall far beyond reality. As magnanimity entails great and noble challenges, it requires action that is fueled by a willingness to serve. The magnanimous manager does not act out of vanity or ambition for recognition that would be unmerited, but with the intention of doing what is good.

In contrast to one who is *pusillanimous*, the magnanimous person does not shy away from doing what he or she considers fit and within his or her ability, with no excessive fear of failure. The magnanimous person is a realist in the companies that he or she takes on, unlike the presumptuous person who launches him or herself at companies which are beyond their powers.

The magnanimous manager is not small-minded, mean or selfish. The magnanimous manager shows complete dedication to the valuable tasks undertaken and values his or her collaborators, making use of their personal and professional qualities and discovering new opportunities for their activity and development.

Magnanimity influences leadership, inspiring trust and serenity, serving as an exemplar of how to overcome dreads and fears. The magnanimous manager will not allow him or herself to be discouraged when difficulties arise, or to fall into sterile complaints, or to yield to anything or anyone in his or her quest to achieve valuable objectives.

Magnanimity will lead on occasion to *magnificence*, spending great sums of money, but appropriately, without extravagance or stinginess. It will also lead to carrying out great schemes to do good for others through important works and companies.

Proactivity

This competency is related to initiating change whenever it might be necessary, rather than reacting to events. It requires wisdom and a sense of responsibility to take charge of circumstances and foreseeable changes, and determination to take opportune decisions early and to do whatever might be fitting. A proactive manager does not wait for something to happen and then adjust him or herself to the new situation, having done nothing beforehand. On the contrary, a proactive manager tries to foresee the future and acts in advance.

Patience

Patience is an important part of the strength that shows itself as an inner power to face and tolerate difficulties without being overcome by sadness or despondency. Patience helps those who have to bear with good spirit the misfortunes and setbacks which appear. At times the events which vex us are of great relevance (a failed business, a prolonged crisis, a change in the economic situation, the announcement of a strike, the illness of a loved one, the news that an essential collaborator is going to a different company...). At other times the events are minor, but more frequent (a fault with technical systems, a delayed flight, lack of time, absence of a secretary, etc.). These can be occasional, but, at times, of long duration.

Patience also helps in dealings with people. Personal faults, differences in personality, ideology or interests can make the interaction difficult. Additionally, the people with whom one works may be affected by a family or personal problem, or simply be in a bad mood, or be demotivated by the job. Or perhaps they may be ill or have lost skills with age, or there might be a thousand other situations which have to be faced. For all of these, patience, so necessary in all contexts of human coexistence, is especially important in the company.

One's own defects and limitations can cause vexation too, so patience is also necessary to come to terms with these and to handle the struggle which emerges from self-knowledge.

A manager with patience tries not to lose his or her calm, keeping his or her spirits up, and not reacting to adversity with surliness or bad temper. Patience helps too in bearing one's own defects and limitations while minded to overcome them, to be understanding with others and to give training to co-workers and subordinates. In contrast, the impatient manager, on losing his or her self-control, wreaks great havoc, loses effectiveness and, above all, fails to improve him or herself.

Constancy

Constancy is steadfastness of mind in resolutions taken. It is related to the implementation of decisions taken, which requires perseverance to pursue goals and continuity in the task undertaken. Constancy is not *obstinacy* in maintaining one's own opinions and being blind to reality. Neither is it a lack of *openness to new ideas* or a lack of willingness to adapt and respond to change. It would not be wise to plough on with old decisions when there is a clear necessity to reconsider them. Constancy means not being fickle when sound resolutions have been taken, and not changing one's mind after hearing every new opinion. Achievements take time and constancy in implementing decisions seems completely necessary. A manager without steadfastness of mind in his or her resolutions would not inspire much confidence.

Order

Order as a virtue means a permanent attitude of situating everything in its correct place and acting properly, giving importance to what is truly important. Order usually makes people more effective, allowing them to make better use of time. Willingness to serve can be manifested in facilitating other people's work through order and providing real leadership by showing in a practical way that one understands it is truly important.

In some cases, order will require a plan of work and the self-discipline to follow it, but order does not necessary mean methodical and strictly programmed work. Sometimes, following a strictly programmed plan will be not possible due to a great variety of tasks or to unforeseen issues or events, as is often the case for managers. In this situation an ordered manager will build order-seeking priorities among this apparent disorder with sound ordination.

Order is evident in *business meetings* in several aspects, including its advance preparation, having a clear purpose, making discussions effective, setting goals during the meeting, then in the appropriate follow-through and assessment of these goals. Order also appears in managers who *organize their own time* well, looking for the right place and time for each activity or assignment, including business trips, which may be quite frequent for many managers. Order is also required in personal grooming, keeping and managing papers and documents, and in personal belongings. These are external expressions of order, but internal order is even more relevant. External order becomes a mere technique when it is not an expression of internal order in one's own ideas and hierarchy of values. When one is not able to order his or her priorities properly, it can cause serious problems to oneself and even to others.

A willingness to learn

Having a willingness to learn is a disposition that favors the acquisition of new information and skills which one sees as potentially appropriate for personal growth and also for serving others. Although this disposition, often also called a *love of learning*, is usually considered only in the educational context, it is actually a moral competency for managers and other professionals. A willingness to learn requires a reflective disposition regarding one's own work to understand and learn how to do things well. Learning can come from others and from personal achievements and even from one's own errors. Studying difficult matters carefully, talking to others and undertaking appropriate training are all expressions of a willingness to learn.

A willingness to learn pushes managers and professionals to keep themselves up to date in their field of expertise, and maybe extending this to take in other related areas, without forgetting the "big picture" of their situation.

A certain *curiosity* is necessary to learn, especially in those matters which affect one's activity, but curiosity can be excessive when its focus is expanded to matters beyond one's brief.

MORAL COMPETENCIES RELATED TO MODERATION

The third spontaneous tendency we are going to consider is the tendency to enjoy what one finds pleasant or comfortable. As with other tendencies, this requires avoiding two extremes: an irrational search of pleasure – sometimes veering toward addiction – on the one hand, and a lack of sensibility for what is enjoyable on the other. Avoiding both extremes in human behavior is the role of another type of moral competencies, which can be grouped together as *moderation*, and which correspond to the classic virtue of *temperance*.

Humility

One can have high or low *self-esteem*. Humility is related to the right level of self-esteem. It comes from self-knowledge, admits qualities and limitations and, consequently, results in acting with realism. Humility can be defined as moderation in personal self-esteem. It is in opposition to the excesses of arrogance, or unrestrained exaltation of one's own excellence – the origin of not a few blunders. It is also far removed from a lack of self-esteem: an unrealistic undervaluing of one's own personality, personal experience or of the prestige one has, and one that can cause certain internal imbalance.

The *arrogant manager* exists wrapped up in his or her own image and reputation; seeking prominence more than the success that authentic professional competence demands. Conserving his or her position is of greater interest than the good of the firm. Conceit leads him or her to underrate others. Not counting much on the talents of anyone else, he or she undervalues the suggestions, comments and contributions of others, and puts little effort into collaborating with their initiatives or into effective teamwork and true participation.

In relations with co-workers the arrogant manager will tend to impose his or her ideas with bullheadedness and intransigence. On occasion, he or she will appreciate the work of subordinates if it serves to highlight his or her own merits. He or she frequently lives shut off from the outside world and has few genuine friends. Arrogance makes everything turn around one's own "I", which becomes the absolute yardstick for reality and, at the extreme, the supreme criterion in judging what is good and what is bad.

In contrast, humility leads the manager to an attitude of self-examination and self-criticism, to listen to others and weigh up their opinions, and recognize one's own errors and reconsider his or her position. Nevertheless, humility does not impede defending one's ideas forcefully, far from it, as not to do so leads one to a posture of acquiescence where error and truth are ranked the same. Precisely by being rooted in the truth humility adds *self-knowledge* to knowledge of the exterior reality. Consequently, the opinions of a modest person are more realistic, and contribute to the creation of a suitable climate for dialogue and the establishment of durable working relations.

A manager with humility has awareness of his or her own merit and dignity and, consistent with this, looks for and accepts posts and assignments for which he or she is capable, but refuses to accept those in which he or she would be incompetent, regardless of the money or prestige such offers might bring.

Humility helps one avoid *delusions of grandeur*, and means one will decline to take on commitments that would be impossible to fulfill. But humility does not prevent one from undertaking great and noble charges (*magnanimity*), or from taking risks, nor does it invite one to happily accept being average. Rather, quite the opposite is the case: a person who knows him or herself is well-positioned to be magnanimous – with realism – and to reap the best benefits possible for all concerned from his or her talents.

Authenticity or "being oneself" is closely related to humility. Leaders with humility base their behavior on what they actually are, not on some questionable self-image.

Diligence

Diligence is a spirited and assiduous application and dedication to work. It is opposed to *laziness*, which is the refusal to make the necessary effort to work or to meet the obligations of one's position or condition. Diligence drives one to conquer weakness, lazy sluggishness and a lack of effectiveness in the use of time.

Diligence leads one to do what is most expedient at all times, not what is most pleasurable. This requires working correctly on what one is doing, with competence and responsibility; not taking the foot off the throttle even when the initial enthusiasm has worn off – finishing things well means continuing to make an effort right to the end. To succeed in this, one has to do what is due, and believe that this is not for the sake of routine or to fill time, nor even for the satisfaction of the work, but for a willingness to serve.

Diligence is also opposed to *activism* in the sense of an immoderate dedication to work. Activism is what we might term "the vice of work". Although it is necessary at times to do a lot of work to meet the pressing needs of the family or firm, at other times there may be an excessive dedication to work and a danger of not attending to one's other obligations. This is a disorder which may have its origin in a disproportionate passion for work, a sense of challenge, or for reasons of greed, vanity, self-affirmation, or even as a way of escaping from the family.

With activism we can find that rather than making use of work to improve oneself, one can end up as a *slave to work*. This is the case of those who surrender themselves to an activity with such frantic absorption that it prevents them listening and attending to others, at times even to their own family about perfectly reasonable matters. The obsession with work that follows from activism can come to cloud the meaning of that very work, and even of life itself. In contrast, an assiduous person works hard, but without allowing him or herself to be enslaved by work. He or she works in a reflective way, pondering the meaning and finality of the work, and harmonizing it with the other aspects of human life. A suitable *work–life balance* helps put work in harmony with other aspects of life, like the family, religious or spiritual activities, sport and so on; this is part of a well-informed diligence.

An orderly agenda is probably a symptom of diligence, and a full diary can also be so, but not if there is no space left for moments of relaxation, or the necessary time for a change of activity. In contrast, a lack of time for reflection is probably a symptom of activism.

Optimistic realism

This is an attitude that makes optimism and realism compatible by looking at the positive side of every situation while maintaining a realistic viewpoint. Optimistic realism is a permanent disposition to overcome pessimistic views or attitudes to see only the negative side of any issue and is acquired through personal effort.

Managers have to be realistic, but realism is not incompatible with presenting the most favorable interpretation of actions and events, or with anticipating the best possible outcome. Optimistic realism requires presenting optimistic views without deception or creating false expectations.

Austerity

Although in economics the idea of austerity is generally associated with a reduction in spending, and especially public spending, austerity as a virtue has a more positive sense, and does not always lead to such cuts. Austerity implies good use of available resources. It is moderation seen as good use of the economic assets, employing them in the best way possible. It runs contrary to excessive restriction on spending as well as wasting money on unnecessary purchases. *Lavishness* can give rise to excessive ostentation or extravagance, which can produce envy and unrest in those who cannot match such spending, especially when the parading of luxury is observed by persons with barely enough to cover the essentials to live.

Austerity induces one to avoid all waste, and to take reasonable advantage of those resources available, without any unnecessary or superfluous spending. An austere manager knows how to spend what is reasonable and fitting as judged by the circumstances of each case, such as taking care of the company image and the standing of the guests at a company event. This virtue makes one attentive to avoiding unnecessary expense on trips, accommodation, restaurants and other situations where squandering can be easy. It is also shown in making energy savings, improving the management of payment collections and in measures to reduce financial overheads, for example.

Liberality in donations

While austerity stimulates attention to avoiding unnecessary expenditure, it is not incompatible with making reasonable donations. The classics referred to making donations reasonably as *liberality*, as they understood the practice "liberates" us from an excessive attachment to money, giving it away generously for the good of others, and with prudence.

Liberality is generosity in making donations and leads us to utilize money opportunely, if it is opportune to give it away. It runs contrary to *miserliness*, which disinclines us to make donations, or permits the practice only at a "miserable level". It runs contrary to *prodigality*, which is a lack of moderation in donations, making them at an unaffordable level, or for unreasonable things, or at the wrong time and place. Moderation in donation means, then, making them with deliberation and effectiveness, without prejudicing the future or the security of the firm, and by contributing effectively to the good of people and society.

Expressions of liberality are, for example, investments to create places of work, or training for people and so on, and donations for appropriate social activities or business patronage.

Anger control

Moderation requires emotional stability. Anger is a well-known emotion and, if it is not moderated, serious distortions of behavior can occur. Like other emotions, such as sadness, fear and joy, anger is an aspect of the human condition which we feel in some circumstances as a spontaneous response to certain behaviors or situations. However, we have the capacity to rationally control these emotions, a capacity which is reinforced through virtues.

The feelings of anger, and in a similar way the sentiments of irritation and indignation, often erupt in response to setbacks or fairly important mishaps. Anger can easily produce a clouding of the reason – one stops thinking with objectivity and serenity – and displays of agression, with the risk of acting improperly and of mistreatment and even violence.

Reacting with force, with temper, to a truly terrible event can be good and necessary. What is not virtuous, though, is to lose control of one's emotions, unloading one's temper on others unfairly or disproportionately. Anger, on being unleashed, produces a strangely satisfying unbridled emotion. But it can be controlled, so that it is only shown when necessary and in appropriate measure. The internal strength for this moderation is known in classical terms as gentleness, corresponding perhaps to "exquisiteness" of treatment of others. This is the "good character" of the person who is capable of controlling his or her anger and annoyance, and not falling into a loss of temper or bad moods. Lack of moderation with anger can lead the manager to unmerited sharpness in relations with others, and even to impose excessively harsh sanctions on them. The emotion of anger stimulates the unfairly harsh penalizing of the performance of subordinates, hence the importance of not taking a decision to find fault with or punish someone without having proper control of one's anger.

Sobriety

Strictly speaking this is the virtue which moderates the consumption of alcoholic drinks. In a wider sense, sobriety can also be applied to moderation in food and, of course, addiction to tobacco and consumption of hallucinogenic drugs. Excessive dedication to hobbies or sports that impacts on one's proper work are also examples of a lack of sobriety.

One can fall into alcoholism not only through an elevated intake, but also through a frequency of consumption. Alcohol prevents lucidity in decision-making, at least temporarily, it reduces work performance, causes accidents and produces difficulties in living together within the family environment. It is the ruin of many young talents, the cause of health problems and an authentic social ill.

Sexual self-control

It may seem odd to include sexual self-control in the competencies for leadership, when in many places society is very permissive, and above all because it is normally considered that sexual practice is a private matter which has no repercussions in the company. Nevertheless, the sexual impulse can become very strong, and when there is no capacity to control it, irrational behavior may appear, and this can have repercussions, not only in the personal and family environment, but also within the firm. Allowing oneself to be led by sexual attraction to a co-worker can result in distortions in the managerial function, favoring the person who is the object of the attention to the detriment of another, or others, who may well have superior merits and competences. More serious still is sexual harassment in the firm, when one is forced to have sexual relations through intimidation, often facilitated by an abuse of power enjoyed by the instigator over the victim. A manager with a lack of sexual moderation fails as a role model, and risks behaving unjustly. Sexual moderation is developed with time; it engenders self-control and the avoidance of situations which might favor sexual intemperance.

INTEGRITY AS COHERENT VIRTUOUS BEHAVIOR

Sometimes integrity is taken as a synonym of honesty (see p. 138) or more often as steadfast adherence to a strict moral code, or even as coherence with one's own values. Others consider integrity as honoring one's own word.[39] However, the genuine meaning of integrity is different. Integrity derives from the Latin *integer*, meaning whole, unbroken, intact and also complete. Integrity in the most genuine sense of the word, then, indicates consistency and moral perfection. Integrity is consistently behaving with moral rectitude in all actions and circumstances. A person with integrity is someone without duplicity, honest and fully virtuous; someone who actively seeks to do good in all circumstances, resisting the temptation of greed for money or power; who does not act in a certain way because it's in fashion, or because others do it, or simply because it appeals. In summary, it is someone who is not "one kind of person in one social context, while quite another in other contexts".[40]

Integrity is being a virtuous person, and this is shown through coherent virtuous behavior. As Robert Solomon affirmed, "integrity is not itself a virtue so much as it is a synthesis of virtues, working together to form a coherent whole".[41] Integrity reminds us, as Aristotle and Aquinas pointed out long ago, that virtues are interrelated and there is a certain *unity of virtues*, at least when they reach a significant degree of maturity. Integrity expresses, therefore, the mutual interrelation and unity to all virtues in people with a high degree of virtue.

Being coherent with one's own values is a necessary condition for integrity, but it is not sufficient. Moral integrity requires a willingness to serve and practical wisdom to align one's own values to authentic ethical values. Otherwise, integrity might easily become obstinacy, being refractory to seek the moral truth.

A manager with integrity is trustworthy. People can trust him or her and have confidence in the consistency and uprightness of his or her behavior over time. That is why integrity is often mentioned as a key competency for leadership.

There are several forms of lack of integrity which erode authority and consequently leadership. A blatant lack of integrity in management would be putting aside ethics to further one's interests or misusing managerial power through means which are illegitimate or immoral.

This is what is generally known as *corruption*; a term which suggests destruction of the wholeness. Apart from this, other forms of a lack of integrity can be found which are particularly relevant in management, including hypocrisy, opportunism and chameleonic behavior.[42]

The etymological meaning of *hypocrisy* is very relevant. In Greek, *hypokrisis* means acting on the stage – pretense. Hypocritical people present themselves as virtuous, or with fake beliefs, feelings or virtues which they do not possess. In short, hypocrisy is a falseness in which there is an appearance of integrity when actually there is not.

In management, hypocrisy can emerge when the exclusive concern is having a good image instead of acting correctly. This led Groucho Marx to quip, "if you can fake that, you've got it made". Integrity is exactly the opposite. That is why developing integrity requires a sincere attitude, avoiding false justifications and searching for what is really good. It also demands examining one's own attitudes and actions before denouncing those of another; avoiding the temptation of seeing a speck in your friend's eye and not the log in your own.

Opportunism concerns exploiting circumstances in self-interest, generally with a lack of regard for moral principles, consequences or others' legitimate interests. In management, there is nothing wrong in taking advantage of any opportunity to achieve legitimate ends; the problem arises when such behavior is carried out with no regard for moral principles or moral hazards.

Power, as well as some organizational or social structures, can foster opportunism. In certain situations economic incentives can also favor opportunistic behavior.

Finally, *chameleonic behavior*. The chameleon is an animal with the unusual ability to change the color of its skin in just a few minutes to help camouflage it or for other reasons. In the context of integrity, chameleons are people with the facility to change their values or principles to adapt themselves to changing circumstances or to please people around them. Adapting oneself to changes in the marketplace or in business is a necessity, as is having flexibility in moving from one culture to another. However, ethical values are objective and moral principles are timeless, and to change these only for interest, fashion or for an easier life runs contrary to integrity. Chameleonic behavior can hardly be compatible with leadership, since followers need to know that a leader will be consistent in his or her behavior. Chameleons cannot be leaders because of their lack of trustworthiness.

EXECUTIVE SUMMARY

The manager, like any other professional, should be competent in his or her specific task of managing and leading organizations. A competent manager should achieve an effective performance,[43] which requires specific competencies. Some are technique-oriented, others are goal-oriented, and a third group includes relation-oriented competencies. There are moral competencies as well, which are rooted in the moral character. They have a direct influence on leadership and probably also an influence on other competencies, especially those which are relation-oriented.

Moral competencies in leadership are nothing other than virtues which provide exemplarity and promote the trust and willingness of people to follow their leader. There are two stable dispositions of character which can be found at the core of the other virtues; namely willingness to serve and practical wisdom. With these as a foundation, a number of virtues are real pillars of leadership. They can be grouped as competencies related to relationability, fortitude and moderation.

Competencies related to relationability strengthen character to eschew acting with egoism and help one to act with respect, care and intelligent love for others. Within this group, it is important to highlight justice and equity, honesty and truthfulness, being committed and loyal to noble causes, care and compassion, kindness, gratitude, forgiveness, solidarity (related to citizenship), stewardship and spirituality.

Competencies related to fortitude regulate the tendency to strive to obtain whatever is seen as valuable, avoiding both disproportionate aggression or passivity. These competencies refer to effort to achieve valuable goals or to resist adversities. Courage, audacity, magnanimity, pro-activity, patience, constancy, order and a willingness to learn stand out.

The tendency to enjoy what one feels as pleasant or comfortable needs moderation (temperance). As with other tendencies, this means avoiding two extremes: an irrational search for pleasure on the one hand, and a lack of sensibility for what is enjoyable on the other. Related to moderation are humility, diligence – which includes an appropriate work–life balance, emotional stability and particularly anger control, optimistic realism, austerity, liberality in donations, sobriety and sexual self-control.

Last, but not least, comes integrity or a harmonious virtuous life, which is shown through coherent virtuous behavior. Integrity expresses the mutual interrelation and unity to all virtues in people with a high degree of virtue and therefore with excellent moral competency.

NOTES AND REFERENCES

Preface

1   This is a different approach from other excellent books on Management Ethics: J. A. Petrick and J. F. Quinn (1997) *Management Ethics. Integrity at Work* (New Delhi: Sage) and N. E. Bowie and P. H. Werhane (2006) *Management Ethics* (Oxford: Blackwell).
2   Some of them can be found in D. Melé (2009) *Business Ethics in Action. Seeking Human Excellence in Organizations* (New York: Palgrave Macmillan).
3   K. H. Blanchard and N. V. Peale (1988) *The Power of Ethical Management* (New York: William Morrow).
4   J. W. Hathaway (1988) 'The Power of Ethical Management (Book Review)', *Business & Society Review*, 64, 79.
5   A. Bhide and H. H. Stevenson (1990) 'Why Be Honest if Honesty Doesn't Pay?', *Harvard Business Review*, 68, 5, 121–129.

Chapter 1

1   O. Sheldon (1923) *The Philosophy of Management* (London: Pitman & Sons) p. ix.
2   In the 1930s, Rowntree's began to develop new brands and marketing. In 1969, the company merged with John Mackintosh & Co. and became known as Rowntree Mackintosh, which was once listed on the London Stock Exchange and was a constituent of the FTSE 100 Index. Finally, in 1988 it was bought by Nestlé.
3   In addition to the above-mentioned book by Sheldon, further details and references can be found at http://en.wikipedia.org/wiki/Oliver_Sheldon and http://en.wikipedia.org/wiki/Rowntree_Company, date accessed 1 September 2011.

4   P. Drucker (1999) *Management Challenges of the 21st Century* (New York: HarperCollins) p. 9.

5   L. Boyer and N. Equilbey (1990) *Histoire du Management* (Paris: Éditions d'Organisation).

6   R. E. Freeman (2000) 'Business Ethics at the Millennium', *Business Ethics Quarterly*, 10, 1, 172.

7   See D. Melé (2005) *Manville Corp., World Leader in the Asbestos Industry (A)*. Case studies BE-159-E and BE-160-E (Barcelona: IESE Publishing).

8   F. W. Taylor (1997) *The Principles of Scientific Management* (Dover Publications, Mineola, NY). First published in 1911 (Harper, New York). See a review in J. Boddewyn (1961) 'Frederick Winslow Taylor Revisited', *The Journal of the Academy of Management*, 2, 100–107.

9   H. Fayol (1984) *General and Industrial Management. Preface of L. Urwick* (Pitman, London). First published in 1916 in French: *Administration Industrielle et Générale; Prévoyance, Organisation, Commandement, Coordination, Controle* (Paris: H. Dunod et E. Pinat).

10 J. P. Kotter (1999) 'What Effective General Managers Really Do', *Harvard Business Review*, 77, 2, 145–159. First published in 1982.

11 H. Mintzberg (2004) *Managers not MBAs: A Hard Look at the Soft Practice of Managing and Management Development* (San Francisco: Berrett-Koehler Publishers).

12 His concern, which we do not discuss here, is that when one leans too far, managing gets out of balance.

13 Science, often considered morally neutral, is not, in fact, since science – even natural science – involves a certain intention and the use of a means (consider, for instance, Nazi medical experimentation).

14 R. T. Pascale and A. G. Athos (1981) *The Art of Japanese Management* (New York: Simon and Schuster).

15 C.-C. Chen and Y.-T. Lee (eds) (2008) *Leadership and Management in China. Philosophies, Theories and Practices* (Cambridge University Press).

16 J. Collins (2001) *Good to Great: Why Some Companies Make the Leap, and Others Don't* (London: Random House).

17 For example, Aristotle most often used the term *ēthē* for character, which is etymologically linked to "ethics" and *morality* (via the Latin equivalent *mores*). (Cf. "Moral Character", *Internet Encyclopedia of Philosophy*: http://www.iep.utm.edu/moral-ch/, date accessed 1 September 2011.)

18 Sheldon, *The Philosophy of Management*, p. 27.

19 See, e.g., I. Hau-siu Chow (2008) 'How Trust Reduces Transaction Costs and Enhances Performance in China's Businesses', *SAM Advanced Management Journal*, 2, 25–34.

20 R. C. Mayer, J. H. Davis and F. D. Schoorman (1995) 'An Integrative Model of Organizational Trust', *Academy of Management Review*, 20, 3, 709–734. See also F. D. Schoorman, R. C. Mayer and J. H. Davis (2007) 'An Integrative Model of Organizational Trust: Past, Present and Future', *Academy of Management Review*, 32, 2, 344–354.

21 Mentioned by R. M. Kramer (2009) 'Rethinking Trust', *Harvard Business Review*, 87, 6, 69.

22 See, e.g., L. Valenzuela, J. Mulki and J. Jaramillo (2010) 'Impact of Customer Orientation, Inducements and Ethics on Loyalty to the Firm: Customers' Perspective', *Journal of Business Ethics*, 93, 2, 277–291; S. Román (2003) 'The Impact of Ethical Sales Behaviour on Customer Satisfaction, Trust and Loyalty to the Company: An Empirical Study in the Financial Services Industry', *Journal of Marketing Management*, 19, 9/10, 915–939.

23 F. Reichheld (1996) *The Loyalty Effect: the Hidden Force Behind Growth, Profits and Lasting Values* (Boston: Harvard Business School Press). See also F. Reichheld (2001) *Loyalty Rules. How Today's Leaders Build Lasting Relationships* (Boston: Harvard Business School Press).

24 See, e.g., S. Hanway (2003) 'Do Layoffs Affect American Workers' Loyalty?' *Gallup Poll Tuesday Briefing*, September 2, 1–3; S. Reinardy (2010) 'Downsizing Effects on Personnel: The Case of Layoff Survivors in U.S. Newspapers', *Journal of Media Business Studies*, 4, 1–19.

25 D. Ross (1925) *Aristotle The Nicomachean Ethics: translated with an Introduction* (Oxford University Press) Book II, Chapter 1.

26 P. H. Werhane and B. Moriarty (2009) *Moral Imagination and Management Decision Making*, p. 10: http://www.darden.virginia.edu/corporate-ethics/pdf/moral_imagination.pdf, date accessed 26 March 2011.

27 M. Yunus (1999) *Banker to the Poor: Micro-Lending and the Battle against World Poverty* (PublicAffairs, New York).

28 R. B. Shaw (1997) *Trust in the Balance. Building Successful Organizations on Results, Integrity and Concern* (San Francisco: Jossey-Bass).

29 E. H. Schein (2010) *Corporate Culture and Leadership*, 4th edn (San Francisco: Jossey-Bass).

30 K. R. Andrews (1989) 'Ethics in Practice', *Harvard Business Review*, 67, 5, 99–104.

31 Ibid., p. 104.

32 J. T. Whetstone (2003) 'The Language of Managerial Excellence: Virtues as Understood and Applied', *Journal of Business Ethics*, 44, 4, 343–357.

Chapter 2

1 F. Michelin (2003) *And Why Not? Morality and Business* (Lanham, MD: Lexington Books) p. 7.
2 Ibid., p. 20.
3 J. R. Rest (1986) *Moral Development: Advances in Research and Theory* (New York: Praeger).
4 These four elements are interrelated but it is our aim here to discuss this complex matter.
5 Plato dealt with virtues in several of his works: see, e.g., I. Vasiliou (2008) *Aiming at Virtue in Plato* (Cambridge University Press, Cambridge, UK). Justice is particularly central in *Republic*: see G. M. A. Grube (translator) (1992) Plato, *Republic, revised by C. D. Reeve* (Indianapolis, IN: Hackett Publishing). Aristotle offers a true treatise of virtues in his *Nicomachean Ethics*: see, e.g., the translation of D. Ross (1925) (Oxford University Press).
6 E. Kant (1998) *Groundwork of the Metaphysics of Morals* (Cambridge, New York). First published in 1785.
7 Alan Ryan, J. S. Mill and J. Bentham (1987) *Utilitarianism and Other Essays* (Penguin, London).
8 M. Scheler (1973) *Formalism in Ethics and Non-formal Ethics of Values: A New Attempt Toward the Foundation of an Ethical Personalism* (Northwester University Press, Evanston, IL). First published in 1913 (vol I) and 1916 (vol II).
9 Merriam-Webster, http://wordcentral.com/cgi-bin/student?book=Student&va=ethics, date accessed 28 May 2011.
10 S. R. Covey (1990) *The Seven Habits of Highly Effective People: Powerful Lessons in Personal Change* (New York: Fireside/Simon & Schuster) p. 35.
11 N. Lopez Moratalla (2010) 'La Búsqueda en el Cerebro de la Dotación Ética Innata y Universal', *Acta Philosophica: Rivista Internazionale di Filosofia*, 19, 2, 297–310.
12 Cf. Covey, op. cit., p. 35, who presents this argument regarding principles.
13 D. Melé (2009) 'Integrating Personalism into Virtue-Based Business Ethics: The Personalist and the Common Good Principles', *Journal of Business Ethics*, 88, 1, 227–244.
14 D. Koehn and A. Leung (2008) 'Dignity in Western versus Chinese Cultures. Theoretical Overview and Practical Illustrations', *Business & Society Review*, 113, 4, 477–504.
15 For a wider discussion, see A. MacIntyre (1993) 'Plain Persons and Moral Philosophy: Rules, Virtues and Goods', *Convivium*, 2nd series, 5, 63–80. Reprinted in: K. Knight (ed.) (1998) *The MacIntyre*

Reader (Cambridge: Polity Press) pp. 136–152. Quotations are from this reprint.

16 We consider that ethical principles are related to human goods and ethical values. However, some authors propose formal principles without any reference to human goods. Here, because of our simplified approach, we do not discuss these other positions, which can be found in any book on theories of ethics.

17 This is the position of the American thinker John Rawls (1971) *A Theory of Justice* (Harvard University Press, Cambridge, MA).

18 Other meanings of love, namely "friendship" (*philia*) and "affection" (*storge*) are not considered here. For a further discussion see C. S. Lewis (1991/1960) *The Four Loves* (Harcourt Brace & Company). First published in 1960.

19 B. Russell (2004) *What I Believe* (London: Routledge). The first edition was published in 1925.

20 Pope Benedict XVI (2009) *Encyclical Letter 'Caritas in Veritate'* (Vatican: Libery Editrice Vatican) §§ 6 and 30. Available at: http://www.vatican.va/holy_father/benedict_xvi/encyclicals/documents/hf_ben-xvi_enc_20090629_caritas-in-veritate_en.html, date accessed 28 July 2011.

21 Literally he says: "intelligence and love are not in separate compartments: *love is rich in intelligence and intelligence is full of love*" (Ibid., § 30). Italics in the original.

22 The Bible, Gospel of Luke 10:25–37. See, e.g., The Holy Bible (1966), *New Revised Standard Version* (Princeton, NJ: Scepter).

23 See, e.g., D. Koehn (1998) *Rethinking Feminist Ethics: Care, Trust and Empathy* (London: Routledge).

24 V. Held (2006) *The Ethics of Care: Personal, Political, Global* (Oxford University Press).

25 A. C. Garnett (1956) 'Charity and Natural Law', *Ethics*, 66, 2, 117–122.

26 Ibid., p. 118.

27 Aristotle, op. cit., Book 8, Chapter 2.

28 See Pope Benedict XVI, op. cit., § 38.

29 Aristotle, op. cit., Book 6, Chapter 5.

30 Aristotle, op. cit., Book 6, Chapter 7.

31 Aristotle, op. cit., Book 6, Chapter 8.

Chapter 3

1 K. R. Andrews (1989) 'Ethics in Practice', *Harvard Business Review*, 67, 5, p. 99.

2   K. R. Andrews (1989) *Ethics in Practice: Managing the Moral Corporation* (Boston, Mass.: Harvard Business School Press).
3   See E. F. Harrison (1999) *The Managerial Decision-making Process*, 5th edn (Boston, Mass.: Houghton Mifflin), p. 37ff.; and the other bibliographical sources mentioned in this work.
4   A. Argandoña (2008) 'Integrating Ethics into Action Theory and Organizational Theory', *Journal of Business Ethics*, 78, 3, 435–446.
5   H. A. Simon (1997/1959) *Administrative Behavior: A Study of Decision-making Processes in Administrative Organizations* (New York: Free Press).
6   M. A. Ariño, J. C. Vazquez-Dodero and S. R. Velamuri (2008) 'Holistic Decision Making and Long Term Firm Performance', *SSRN*, http://ssrn.com/abstract=1263786, date accessed 1 September 2011. These authors suggested that decisions involving interactions with stakeholders have three impact dimensions in decision-making: a) *effectiveness* b) *operative learning* and c) *relational learning*, which are closely related with our instrumental, internal and relational dimensions. In their approach, however, the ethical dimension remains implicit.
7   CNN.com (2 September 2002), http://archives.cnn.com/2002/BUSINESS/asia/09/02/japan.tepco/index.html, accessed 5 August 2011.
8   G. Bernanos (1955) *'Why Freedom?' The Last Essays of Georges Bernanos* (Chicago, IL: Henry Regnery).
9   Merriam-Webster, http://www.merriam-webster.com/dictionary/bribe, date accessed 5 August 2011.

Chapter 4

1   P. F. Drucker (1990) *The New Realities* (London: Mandarin) p. 221.
2   C. I. Barnard (1968/1938) *The Functions of the Executive. Introduction of K. Andrews* (London: Oxford University Press) p. 8.
3   H. Simon (1985) 'Human Nature in Politics: The Dialogue of Psychology with Political Science', *American Political Science Review of Business*, 79, p. 293.
4   A. Sen (1987) *On Ethics and Economics* (Oxford: Blackwell Publishing).
5   J. E. Stiglitz (1994) *Whither Socialism?* (Cambridge, MA: MIT Press).
6   Interview with J. E. Stiglitz in Beppe Grillo's Blog (2007): http://www.beppegrillo.it/eng/2007/01/stiglitz.html, date accessed 5 August 2011.
7   S. Ghoshal (2005) 'Bad Management Theories Are Destroying Good Management Practices', *Academy of Management Learning*

& *Education*, 4, 1, 75–91. See other authors' arguments on this issue.

8   In the theological context angels are also persons and God is a personal being. They are rational subjects but not rational animals. Some authors have extended the concept of person to some animals which show a certain intelligence (but not conceptual or discursive thought), while others deny that unborn human beings are persons. Here we will use person as being synonymous with the human being.

9   The German philosopher Robert Spaemann (2006) provided a serious study of this difference in *Persons: The Difference between `Someone' and `Something'* (Oxford and New York: Oxford University Press).

10   D. Ross (1925) *Aristotle The Nicomachean Ethics* (Oxford University Press) I, 13.

11   Sellers generally have much more information than buyers or consumers, and can abuse such power in deceit and fraud when selling their products. In doing so, they take advantage of consumer ignorance, or their lack of means to verify the information provided by a seller.

12   Abuse, from the Latin *abusus* (rooted in *abusi*, *ab-* "away" and *uti* "use"), when applied to people means improper usage of people or treating them for a bad purpose.

13   Companies who adopt UN Global Compact are committed to embrace, support and enact, within their sphere of influence, ten principles. These derived from a number of documents of the United Nations, including The Universal Declaration of Human Rights, The International Labor Organization's Declaration on Fundamental Principles and Rights at Work, The Rio Declaration on Environment and Development, and The United Nations Convention Against Corruption.

14   Academy of Management (2010), http://annualmeeting. aomonline.org/2010/, date accessed 6 August 2011.

15   This follows partially the rational of the Academy of Management (2010). See previous note for the link.

16   Online Etymology Dictionary, http://www.etymonline.com/ index.php?search=organization&searchmode=none, date accessed 6 August 2011.

17   J. P. R. French Jr. and B. Raven (1960) 'The Bases of Social Power' in D. Cartwright and A. Zander (eds) *Group Dynamics* (New York: Harper and Row) pp. 607–623.

18   B. George (2007) 'Nonperforming CEOs', *BusinessWeek Online*, 7 Sept.

19   Ibid.

20 M. Huselid (1995) 'The Impact of Human Resource Management Practices on Turnover, Productivity, and Corporate Financial Performance', *Academy of Management Journal*, 38, 3, 635–72.
21 See J. A. Pérez López (2002) *Fundamentos de la Dirección de Empresas*, 5th edn (Madrid: Rialp), who I am following partially in this point.
22 D. Melé and J. M. Rosanas (2003) 'Power, Freedom and Authority in Management: Mary Parker Follett's "Power-With", *Philosophy of Management*, 3, 2, pp. 35–46.
23 C. Heckscher (1995) 'The Failure of Participatory Management', *Across the Board*, 32, 10, 16–21.
24 D. Melé (2005) 'Exploring the Principle of Subsidiarity in Organizational Forms', *Journal of Business Ethics*, 60, 3, 293–305.

Chapter 5

1   A. H. Van de Ven (2001) 'Medtronic's Chairman William George on How Mission-driven Companies Create Long-term Shareholder Value', *Academy of Management Executive*, 15, 4, 39–47.
2   W. W. George (2003) *Authentic Leadership: Rediscovering the Secrets to Creating Lasting Value* (San Francisco: Jossey-Bass) p. 35.
3   It is guidance for private and public sector organizations of all types based on an international consensus among expert representatives of the main stakeholder groups.
4   UN World Commission on Environment and Development (1987) *Our Common Future* (Oxford University Press).
5   See S. A. Waddock, C. Bodwell and S. B. Graves (2002) 'Responsibility: The New Business Imperative', *Academy of Management Executive*, 16, 2, 132–148.
6   See, e.g., M. C. Jensen (2001) 'Value Maximization, Stakeholder Theory, and the Corporate Objective Function', *European Financial Management*, 7, 3, 297–317.
7   D. W. Greening and D. B. Turban (2000) 'Corporate Social Performance as a Competitive Advantage in Attracting Quality Workforce', *Business and Society*, 39, 3, 254–280.
8   C. Handy (1997) 'The Citizen Corporation', *Harvard Business Review*, 75, 5, 28.
9   M. Friedman (1970) 'The Social Responsibility of Business is to Increase its Profits', *New York Times Magazine*, 13 Sept. 32–33, 122, 126.
10 "In such an economy", wrote Milton Friedman with his wife Rose, "there is one and only one social responsibility of business –

to use resources and engage in activities designed to increase its profits so long as it stays within the rules of the game, which is to say, engages in open and free competitions, without deception or fraud." (M. Friedman and R. Friedman (1962) *Capitalism and Freedom* (Chicago: University of Chicago Press) p. 133.)

11 W. Lazonick and M. O'Sullivan (2000) 'Maximizing shareholder value: a new ideology for corporate governance', *Economy and Society*, 29, 1, 13–35. For a sound criticism see J. Fontrodona and A. J. G. Sison (2006) 'The Nature of the Firm, Agency Theory and Shareholder Theory: A Critique from Philosophical Anthropology', *Journal of Business Ethics*, 66, 1, 33–42.

12 M. C. Jensen (2001) op. cit.

13 See R. E. Freeman (2004) 'A Stakeholder Theory of the Modern Corporation' in T. L. Beauchamp and N. E. Bowie (eds) *Ethical Theory and Business* (Upper Saddle River, NJ: Pearson-Prentice Hall); and R. E. Freeman, J. S. Harrison, A. C. Wicks, B. L. Parmar and S. de Colle (2010) *Stakeholder Theory: The State of the Art* (New York: Cambridge University Press).

14 R. E. Freeman (1984) *Strategic Management: A Stakeholder Approach* (Boston: Pitman). A new edition is also available (New York: Cambridge University Press, 2010).

15 Merck, http://www.merck.com/about/mission.html, date accessed 6 August 2011.

16 T. Donaldson and L. E. Preston (1995) 'The Stakeholder Theory of the Corporation: Concepts, Evidence, and Implications', *Academy of Management Review*, 20, 1, 65–91.

17 R. E. Freeman (1999) 'Divergent Stakeholder Theory', *Academy of Management Review*, 24, 2, 233–236.

18 B. R. Agle, T. Donaldson, R. E. Freeman, M. C. Jensen, R. K. Mitchell and D. J. Wood (2008) 'Dialogue: Towards Superior Stakeholder Theory', *Business Ethics Quarterly*, 18, 2, 153–190.

19 A. Argandoña (2011) 'Stakeholder Theory and Value Creation', *Working Paper WP-922*, IESE Business School.

20 A. Argandoña (1998) 'The Stakeholder Theory and the Common Good', *Journal of Business Ethics*, 17, 1093–1102.

21 T. L. Fort (1996) 'Business as Mediating Institution', *Business Ethics Quarterly*, 6, 2, 149–164. T. L. Fort (2001) *Ethics and Governance: Business as Mediating Institution* (Oxford University Press: Ruffin Series in Business Ethics).

22 J. Pfeffer (2010) 'Building Sustainable Organizations: The Human Factor', *Academy of Management Perspectives*, 24, 1, 34–45.

23 Ibid., p. 43.

24 Our approach to corporate citizenship is similar to that given by the 2002 World Economic Forum in New York. In the document

'Global Corporate Citizenship – the Leadership Challenge for CEOs and Boards' we read: "Corporate citizenship is about the contribution a company makes to society through its core business activities, its social investment and philanthropy programs, and its engagement in public policy."

25 M. E. Porter and M. R. Kramer (2006) 'Strategy & Society: The Link Between Competitive Advantage and Corporate Social Responsibility', *Harvard Business Review*, 84, 12, 78–92.

Chapter 6

1 C. I. Barnard (1968/1938) *The Functions of the Executive. Introduction by K. Andrews* (London: Oxford University Press) p. 282.

2 Ibid., p. 258.

3 Ibid., pp. 258–9.

4 A. Zaleznik (1977) 'Managers and Leaders: Are They Different?', *Harvard Business Review*, 55, 3, 67–78.

5 R. Boyatzis (1982) *The Competent Manager: A Model for Effective Performance* (New York: John Wiley & Sons).

6 D. C. McClelland (1973) 'Testing for Competencies Rather Than Intelligence', *American Psychologist*, 28, 1, 1–14.

7 See, e.g., E. E. Lawler III (1994) 'From Job-based to Competency-based Organizations', *Journal of Organizational Behavior*, 15, 1, 3–5.

8 P. Cardona (2005) *Cómo Desarrollar las Competencias de Liderazgo* (Pamplona: Eunsa); S. Schlebusch and G. Roodt (2008) *Assessment Centres; Unlocking Potential for Growth* (Randburg, South Africa: Knowres Publishing (Pty) Ltd.); G. C. Thornton III, W. C. Byham and P. Warr (1982) *Assessment Centers and Management Performance* (New York: Academic Press).

9 These and the following lists of competencies are taken from different authors (see note 8) and it is only tentative. Our purpose is merely to discuss moral competencies in accordance with the title of this chapter.

10 J. Brownell (2006) 'Meeting the Competency Needs of Global Leaders: A Partnership Approach', *Human Resource Management*, 45, 3, 309–333, mentioning several authors on p. 310.

11 Y. Sankar (2003) 'Character Not Charisma is the Critical Measure of Leadership', *Journal of Leadership & Organizational Studies*, 9, 4, 45–55.

12 P. Drucker (2005) *The Practice of Management* (Oxford: Elsevier) p. 155.

13 H. Mintzberg (2004) *Managers Not MBAs: A Hard Look at the Soft Practice of Managing and Management Development* (San Francisco: Berrett-Koehler Publishers).

14 B. M. Bass and P. Steidlmeier (1999) 'Ethics, Character, and Authentic Transformational Leadership Behavior', *The Leadership Quarterly*, 10, 2, 181–217.

15 Brownell, op. cit., p. 310.

16 J. B. Ciulla (ed.) (1998) *Ethics, the Heart of Leadership* (New York: Praeger).

17 A. J. G. Sison (2003) *The Moral Capital of Leaders. Why Virtue Matters* (Cheltenham, UK and Northampton, MA, USA: Edward Elgar).

18 A. Kolp and P. Rea (2006) *Leading with Integrity: Character-Based Leadership* (Cincinnati, OH: Atomic Dog Publishers).

19 K. R. Andrews (1989) 'Ethics in Practice', *Harvard Business Review*, 67, 5, pp. 99–104.

20 D. J. Moberg (2000) 'Role Models and Moral Exemplars: How Do Employees Acquire Virtues by Observing Others?', *Business Ethics Quarterly*, 10, 3, 675–696.

21 M. Neubert, D. S. Carlson, K. M. Kacmar, J. Roberts and L. B. Chonko (2009) 'The Virtuous Influence of Ethical Leadership Behavior: Evidence from the Field', *Journal of Business Ethics*, 90, 157–170; M. E. Brown and L. K. Treviño (2003) 'Influence of Leadership Styles on Unethical Conduct in Work Groups', Academy of Management Proceedings, pp. B1–B6.

22 B. M. Bass and P. Steidlmeier, op. cit.

23 R. K. Greenleaf (2002) *Servant Leadership. A Journey into the Nature of Legitimate Power and Greatness* (New York: Paulist Press).

24 R. K. Greenleaf, op. cit.; M. De Pree (1990) *Leadership is an Art* (New York: Dell Books); P. Senge (1990) *The Fifth Discipline: The Art and Practice of the Learning Organization* (New York: Doubleday); S. Covey (1991) *Principle-Centered Leadership* (New York: Summit Books); and J. C. Hunter (1998) *The Servant: A Simple Story About the True Essence of Leadership* (Roseville, California: Prima Publishing).

25 J. A. Pérez López (2002) *Fundamentos de la Dirección de Empresas* (Madrid: Rialp) Ch. 8. See also J. A. Pérez López (1998) *Liderazgo y Ética en la Dirección de Empresas. La Nueva Empresa del Siglo XXI* (Bilbao: Deusto).

26 J. A. Pérez López, *Liderazgo y Ética en la Dirección de Empresas* p. 97ff.

27 D. Ross (1925) *Aristotle The Nicomachean Ethics* (Oxford University Press) Book 6, Chapter 12.

28 M. Novak (1996) *Business as a Calling – Work and the Examined Life* (New York: The Free Press).

29 For a more detailed explanation, see C. Llano (1991) *El Empresario ante la Responsabilidad y la Motivación* (México: McGraw-Hill).

30 C. R. Solomon (1999) *A Better Way to Think About Business: How Personal Integrity Leads to Corporate Success* (New York: Oxford University Press) p. 91. Honesty, etymologically, has to do with honor. Consequently, dishonesty is related to shame, probity and honorableness. However, honesty is often understood as being truthful. Thus, an honest person is one who tells the truth, and does not lie.

31 Ibid.

32 P. Frost (2003) *Toxic Emotions at Work: How Compassionate Managers Handle Pain and Conflicts* (Cambridge, MA: Harvard Business School Press).

33 J. E. Dutton, M. C. Worline, P. J. Frost and J. Lilius (2006) 'Explaining Compassion Organizing', *Administrative Science Quarterly*, 51, 1, 159–96.

34 C. Peterson and M. Seligman (2004) *Character Strengths and Virtues: A Handbook and Classification* (Washington, DC: American Psychological Association) p. 446.

35 K. Cameron and R. F. Caza (2002) 'Organizational and Leadership Virtues and the Role of Forgiveness', *Journal of Leadership & Organizational Studies*, 9, 33–48.

36 Online Etymology Dictionary, http://www.etymonline.com/index.php?term=solidarity, date accessed 31 May 2011.

37 John Paul II, *Letter Encyclical 'Sollicitudo Rei Socialis'*, n. 38. Available at: http://www.vatican.va/edocs/ENG0223/__P6.HTM, date accessed 31 May 2011.

38 C. Peterson and M. Seligman, op. cit., p. 370.

39 W. Erhard, M. C. Jensen and S. Zaffron (2009) 'Integrity: A Positive Model that Incorporates the Normative Phenomena of Morality, Ethics and Legality', *Harvard Business School*, Working Paper No. 06-11, 23 March. Available at SSRN, http://ssrn.com/abstract=920625, date accessed 31 May 2011.

40 A. MacIntryre (1999) 'Social Structures and Their Threats to Moral Agency', *Philosophy*, 74, 3, p. 317.

41 C. R. Solomon, op. cit., p. 38.

42 Ibid., pp. 40–3.

43 R. Boyatzis (1982) *The Competent Manager: A Model for Effective Performance* (New York: John Wiley & Sons).

AUTHOR'S INDEX

Q

Quinn, J.J. vii (*note 1*)

R

Raven, B. 89 (*note 17*)
Rawls, J. 34 (*note 17*)
Rea, P. 132
Reichheld, F. 15 (*note 23*)
Reinardy, S. 16 (*note 24*)
Rest, J. 24
Roberts, J. 133 (*note 21*)
Román, S. 15 (*note 22*)
Roodt, G. 130 (*note 8*)
Rosanas, J.M. 94 (*note 22*)
Russell, B. 38

S

Sankar, Y. 132
Schein, E.H. 19 (*note 29*)
Scheler, M. 27
Schlebusch, S. 130 (*note 8*)
Schoorman, F.D. 14 (*note 20*)
Seligman, M. 141 (*note 34*), 142
   (*note 38*)
Sen, A. 75
Shaw, R.B. 18 (*note 28*)
Sheldon, O. 1, 13
Simon, H.A. 50, 74
Sison, A. 111 (*note 11*), 132
Socrates 34
Solomon, C.R. 138 (*note 30*), 153
Spaemann, R. 75 (*note 9*)
Steidlmeier, P. 132 (*note 14*), 134
   (*note 22*)
Stevenson, H.H. viii (*note 5*)

Stiglitz, J.E. 75
Stuart Mill, J. 27
Sun Tzu 90

T

Taylor, F. 8, 73
Thornton III, G.C. 130 (*note 8*)
Treviño, L.K. 133 (*note 21*)
Turban, D.B. 106 (*note 7*)

V

Valenzuela, L. 15 (*note 22*)
Van de Ven, A.H. 101 (*note 1*)
Vasiliou, I. 26 (*note 5*)
Vazquez-Dodero, J.C. 50 (*note 6*)
Velamuri, S.R. 50 (*note 6*)

W

Waddock, S.A. 105 (*note 5*)
Warr, P. 130 (*note 8*)
Werhane, P.H. vii (*note 1*), 18
   (*note 26*)
Whetstone, J.T. 19 (*note 32*)
Wood, D.J. 112 (*note 18*)
Worline, M.C. 139 (*note 33*)

Y

Yunus, M. 18

Z

Zaffron, S. 153 (*note 39*)
Zaleznik, A. 129

SUBJECT INDEX